The Art of the Party

DESIGN IDEAS FOR SUCCESSFUL ENTERTAINING

RENNY REYNOLDS

TEXT BY ELAINE LOUIE ▪ *PHOTOGRAPHS BY EDWARD ADDEO*

Gibbs Smith, Publisher
Salt Lake City

First published in 1992
by Viking Penguin, a division of Penguin Books USA Inc.

Reprinted in 2003 by Gibbs Smith, Publisher
07 06 05 04 03   5 4 3 2 1

Published by
Gibbs Smith, Publisher
P.O. Box 667
Layton, Utah 84041

Orders: (1-800) 748-5439
www.gibbs-smith.com

Interior design by Joseph Rutt
Printed and bound in Tokyo

Library of Congress Cataloging-in-Publication Data

Reynolds, Renny.
   Art of the party / Renny Reynolds, Elaine Louie.— 1st ed.
       p. cm
   Originally published: New York, NY: Viking, 1992.
   ISBN 1-58685-249-3
   1. Entertaining. I. Louie, Elaine. II. Title

   TX731 .R45 2003
   642'.4—dc21   2002030618

Acknowledgments

■ ■ ■ ■ ■ ■ ■ ■ ■ ■ ■ ■ ■ ■ ■ ■ ■

Putting together a book takes a great amount of cooperation on the part of a large number of people—particularly a book like this, which was photographed at more than forty different locations, many of them private homes. Often the photographs needed to be taken at the last minute before the guests entered the party, requiring great patience on the part of hostesses, party planners, caterers, and others.

Elaine Louie and I would like to extend our sincere appreciation to Brooke Astor, Anne Bass, Carol Berliner, Glenn Birnbaum, Steve Cramer, Ray Frankel, Stephanie French and Amory Houghton, Edward and Arlyn Gardner, Hazel Haire, Robert Homma, Martha Hyder, Yue-Sai Kan, Anne Livet, Sue and Frederick Menowitz, Susan and Donald Newhouse, Dailey Pattee, Gail Perl, Robert Richie, Harriette Rose-Katz, Louisa Sarofim, Kenny Scharf, Anne and Herbert Siegel, Sandy Sobel, Ivana Trump, Barbara Walters, Sylvia Weinstock, Peter Wolf, and Ann Viccaro.

And a million thanks to all the gang at Renny who help produce all our parties: Pat McCoy, Denise Akire, Rick Baumann, Daniel Aristumo, Carlos Porto, David Roberson, Theresa Murphy, and Miriam Rivera.

—R. R.

CONTENTS

INTRODUCTION

■ ■

Parties celebrate the most important moments of life—a birthday, an anniversary, a wedding. The best parties reflect your own unique style and taste and reveal your generosity of spirit as a host. I also feel that parties should have a sense of largesse and drama—glamour, if you will. A truly glamorous party expands your sense of what is beautiful and enlarges your vision of what endless possibilities there are to the simple notion of fun.

At a party, the senses should be tickled, provoked, heightened. Exciting the senses usually involves exaggeration. Centerpieces that soar twelve feet above the table emphasize the scale. Scattered diamond dust on a sidewalk transforms an ordinary street into a glittering path. Gardenias tucked into a centerpiece make a room fragrant and suggest romance. Parties should be wildly sensuous, but the trick is to carefully consider both the space where the party is to be held and your own personality.

First, figure out what type of party you want. Do you want a formal seated dinner or a casual buffet on a lawn? Are you comfortable with an avant-garde beach theme that perhaps includes half-naked young men posing as lifeguards, or is the serene good taste of tables set with silver candelabra, damask tablecloths, and champagne roses more your style? To execute any party design, whether it is big or small, formal or informal, I use five design elements—lighting, color, texture, progression, and scale—as the basis for creating dramatic parties.

■ ■ ■ ■ ■ ■ ■ ■ ■ ■ ■ ■

■ ■

Lighting may be the single most important design element. If the lighting is wrong, the most dramatic or subtle design can be lost. If you fill a four-story ballroom with thousands of yards of silk ribbons crisscrossing the room diagonally, you must have shafts of light shooting through these ribbons, pointing up their color and angle, so that guests are dazzled by the brilliant colors shooting across the ceiling. If you have created six-foot centerpieces of champagne roses, lavender delphinium, and pale pink lilies, and they're not lit by candlelight or a spotlight, the eye will ignore the flowers. Instead, the eye will travel to other areas of the room— chandeliers, sconces, and any other sources of light in the dark space.

Color can emphasize the theme of a party and help create the mood. What would a Mexican party be without bright colors like hot pink, turquoise, orange, and purple? Those same colors would be totally inappropriate for most weddings. We think of weddings as white or pale, pastel-colored events—soft and romantic. Black and white, in combination, evoke the glamorous era of Fred Astaire and Ginger Rogers, he in black tux, she in white chiffon, dancing on a black-and-white-checkered dance floor.

Texture is another important element that sets the style and tone of a party. Texture, whether it's in the tablecloth, the napkin, or the centerpiece, makes you feel extremely sensuous. Your senses of touch and smell may be heightened. A copper

metallic tablecloth is not only a departure from the linen tablecloth, but it also has a silky gauzy touch and, above all, reflects light. A topiary centerpiece made of fruit and flowers can be even more tactile if a halved pomegranate is included, exposing the red-seeded white flesh against the dark red leathery skin. Try including clusters of black, burgundy, and green grapes cascading onto the table, and among the fruit scatter roses and freesias.

Some of the most exciting parties are those that progress from one space to another, for cocktails, dinner, dessert, and dance. These parties are like theater. There is a beginning, middle, and end. Parties can progress from one indoor space to another—a foyer for cocktails, a dining room for dinner, the living room for dessert. Outdoors, a party can be designed around the setting of the sun. At dusk, guests can wander, cocktails in hand, through a rose garden. As the sun goes down, garden torches light up, and dinner can be served at a table facing the ocean. By changing the vistas, the guests are never bored. The rose garden affects their sense of smell. The expansive view of the ocean is relaxing, while the scent of the salt air is bracing.

Scale is also a crucial design element. Most people are afraid of huge scale, just as they are afraid of color. But visual drama is a major component of a party. In a four-story ballroom, twelve-foot-high centerpieces fill the empty space, focus the guests' attention, and add startling drama to what could be a cavernous space. Scale can also take the form of figuring out how many candles are needed to decorate a table, or how wide the streamers should be when they are designed to flutter over the tables. When designing parties, do not be afraid of exaggerating the size and scale of the design elements—flowers, candles, ribbons, lights.

In twenty years of designing parties, I've had the great fun of working in some of the most beautiful spaces in the country—and also some of the most unattractive. There is no space that cannot be transformed into a place of magic. The ideas in this book can all be translated to your needs, but the best use of this book is to take these ideas as points of reference, and then let your imagination take over.

LIGHTING

■ ■

L ighting creates mood, drama, illusion. Each kind of light—candles, spot-lights, tiny white Christmas lights, theatrical projection lights or spotlights—evokes a different atmosphere. If the lighting is not right, and fails to create a feeling of drama, romance, or mystery, a party can fail. The atmosphere will become mundane rather than joyous. People may find themselves swallowed by dark shadows or blinded by glare, rather than bathed in warm, gentle pools of light.

We often rent theatrical spotlights to create a highly dramatic mood. To vary the intensity of the light, we use colored gels on the spotlights. A gel is a heat-tolerant piece of plastic that attaches to the spotlight. There are as many different colored gels to choose from as there are colors in the spectrum. Gel paper, which is available from any stage lighting supply store, can be placed over the simplest uplight or downlight used in the home. By mixing color and light, we can achieve a myriad of effects. Shoot a beam of light, masked by a red gel, on a topiary of red roses. Shoot another beam of light, covered by a yellow gel, on a topiary of yellow roses. The effect? By matching the color of the gel to that of the roses, the natural colors of the flowers are heightened.

Of all the kinds of lighting, candlelight is most synonymous with romance. The warm golden light masks wrinkles and makes people feel serene rather than harried. The votive candle is ubiquitous for a reason—it throws light up onto faces.

■ ■

Combine tall candles with low candles, and the entire room glows.

A dark eighteenth-century dining room, with wood beams and a stone fireplace, came alive with slender tapers in an eighteenth-century tin chandelier and low pillar candles on the table. To make the room look as large as it is, and the guests feel more expansive and aware of the sense of space, we also placed an uplight with a pale pink spotlight in each corner.

In the Waldorf-Astoria ballroom in Manhattan, we filled the cavernous ceiling with hundreds of tiny white Christmas lights. Guests who succumbed to a suspension of disbelief thought they were dancing under the stars.

To amuse an eighty-year-old woman at her birthday party, we lit the tables with transparent tubes of colorful electric lights. For people who were used to dining by candlelight, the flickering lights were a new form of illumination.

In an outdoor tent party, we created drama on the fabric ceiling by using theatrical projection lamps and templates. As guests looked up at the ceiling, they saw a random design of twisting, curving branches.

Narrow-beam spotlights are often used to pinpoint and highlight a center-piece. But for a party in Texas, we built boxes with spotlights shining from below the centerpieces. The effect of this lighting was that it looked as if the flowers were emanating light. Because the light source was invisible, a sense of mystery was created.

A Night in the Stars

▪ ▪ ▪ ▪ ▪ ▪ ▪ ▪ ▪ ▪ ▪ ▪ ▪ ▪ ▪ ▪

This party was held in the cavernous four-story Grand Ballroom of the Waldorf-Astoria Hotel in New York City. To fill the void over the heads of the guests, we designed a shimmering canopy of light.

For the party, a benefit for the Weizmann Institute of Science, we hung 120 strands of tiny white Christmas tree lights, which, for variety and visual interest, varied in length from thirty-five to fifty feet, and held either thirty-five, fifty, or one hundred lights spaced six inches apart. The lights were attached to twenty cables that were, in turn, fastened to the chandelier and stretched across the ceiling to the balustrades on the balcony.

Because the lights were so tiny, we also hung 250 large silver stars for drama. Just as the strands of lights were different lengths, so were the stars different sizes. Some were six inches in diameter, and the rest were ten.

Since we had transformed the room into an evening sky lit by stars, we covered the tables with midnight-blue cotton tablecloths and scattered seven white votive candles on each table. Thirty-inch-high vases were filled with white dendrobium orchids and six-foot-high branches of curly willow. Silver ribbons, three to four feet in length, were knotted to the willow branches so that they reflected light from both the Christmas lights and the candles.

The canopy of lights gave the impression of a vast night sky stretching endlessly into space. Wherever the guests looked, there were glimmers of light. People were engulfed in the illusion of a Milky Way.

A shimmering curtain of light reflects off the white flowers at this party, held in a grand hotel ballroom.

LEFT: Tiny white lights twinkle behind tall vases, which are filled with white dendrobium orchids and curly willow branches.

RIGHT: A spotlight focuses on the centerpiece of each table, and the lights in the chandelier are covered by red, green, and blue gels.

Dinner at the Asia Society

■ ■ ■ ■ ■ ■ ■ ■ ■ ■ ■ ■ ■ ■ ■ ■

At the Asia Society, a modern brick building on Manhattan's Park Avenue, where cultural events—films, concerts, lectures—on Asia are offered, we designed a party for the Asian International Film Festival. Because there were two hundred guests, we had to decorate an assortment of rooms, including some not normally used for parties. Some rooms had walls covered with beige-colored raw silk and left beautifully spare and unadorned. Other rooms, however, were hung—actually cluttered—with portraits of benefactors of the society. Some rooms had high ceilings, others low ceilings. We wanted the design of the party to be consistent throughout the rooms. The solution was to have at every table the same elaborate centerpiece, where light—masses of white lanterns lit by candlelight—was the unifying and dominant element.

In the center of each of the long rectangular tables, there was a three-foot-high vase filled with seven-foot-high curly willow branches, white dendrobium orchids, and white Casablanca lilies. From the willow branches we hung eight-inch-high white paper lanterns tied with black ribbons. Each lantern was lit with a white votive candle, which was placed in a glass container, which in turn fit snugly into the plastic holder at the bottom of the lantern. Because these arrangements were so huge in scale and so aromatic and romantic-looking, they dominated the room.

Because the normally bright lights in the rooms couldn't be dimmed, they were not used; instead the lanterns became the major light source. Their soft glow unified the rooms.

For continuity of design, the black-and-white theme of this dinner is repeated in the tablecloths as well as in the lanterns.

ABOVE: The sculptural quality of curly willow branches, highlighted by the lanterns, creates an effect similar to that achieved in Japanese flower design. We also use branches because they cast dramatic shadows.

LEFT: The room is lit on two levels: the lanterns illuminate the overhead space and the votive candles brighten the table.

RIGHT: For parties, votive candles that last ten hours are a must.

The black-and-white color scheme, which was hinted at in the flower and lantern design, was made bold in the table settings. The tables were alternately set with either a black tablecloth topped with white napkins and white plates, or a white tablecloth topped with black napkins and black plates. Chairs were black with white moiré cushions. The starkness of the black-and-white scheme contrasted with the texture and fragrant seductiveness of the flower and lantern design.

ABOVE: Along the tables at this birthday party, Italian stone pots hold a mix of roses, tuberoses, and jasmine. Candles at different heights make spots of light appear scattered, not straight, at the long table.

Dinner by the Bay

Only the light of candles and the setting sun illuminated this birthday dinner party for twenty-four in Southampton at a house whose porch overlooked Lake Agawam.

The party began at 8:00 P.M. as the sun was beginning to set. Guests strolled through the garden, enjoying the scent of roses, lavender, and lilies and listening to the sounds of a frog croaking in the distance. As the sun sank lower, waiters scurried around lighting dozens and dozens of candles and torches. By 9:00 P.M., when dinner was served, the entire landscape was visible solely by firelight.

Mounted around the lake were twenty-four Tiki torches, each of which stood six feet high. Around the garden, there were four-foot-high stakes topped with hurricane lamps holding white candles. Four dozen more hurricane lamps lit the way from the driveway through the garden and across the lawn to the porch, where dinner was held.

ABOVE: From table to gardens to pool, torches as well as tapers—large flames and small—light the party.

ABOVE LEFT: This Victorian beach house in Southampton, New York, is surrounded by perennial gardens. For drama, simple garden torches, scattered throughout the flower beds, are lit at dusk.

The long table, eighteen feet long and four feet wide, was covered with an undercloth of French blue linen and an overcloth of handmade white linen openwork lace. To break up such a long table, we divided the flowers and candles into six groupings. In that way guests were made to feel cozier, as if they were at their own small party.

For every grouping of six, there were two large hurricane lamps, eight inches and twelve inches high, casting

wide pools of light. Made in Murano, Italy, the lamps had swirls of white glass that made the light seem slightly distorted and, at the same time, magnified. Just as there was an excess of candlelight, so too there was a splendid abundance of flowers. For twenty-four people, there were twenty-eight miniature Italian terra-cotta pots filled with blue and cream-colored hydrangeas, peach garden roses, pale pink and lavender sweet peas, and heavily scented white tuberoses and jasmine. Because there were more pots of flowers than there were guests, there was a feeling of luxury at the table. The scents of the flowers mingled with the smells of the garden and the ocean air. (If the party were held indoors, however, the combination of scents might be too strong and overwhelm the aromas of the food.)

To end the dinner, there was a brief musicale. A white upright piano had been placed on the porch and as the pianist began to play, young opera singers, students at the Juilliard School of Music, walked onto the lawn and began to sing Puccini arias. The light from the moon, torches, and candles created a theatrical setting for the musical coda to the evening.

A New Wave Texas Dinner

For a dinner preceding a ball in Houston, Texas, we wanted to highlight flowers in ways seldom seen. We designed centerpieces in which flowers were submerged in water and magnified by lighting. The result was almost surreal.

To achieve this effect, we placed the flowers in clear fishbowl vases filled to the brim with water, just one drop short of spilling over. Then we lit the vases from beneath using twelve-inch-square black-painted pine lightboxes. Inside each box, which was lined with a thin sheet of aluminum so it wouldn't burn, we placed two five-inch twenty-five-watt tubular bulbs. The box was covered with a black plastic grid through which the light shone. To soften the hard edges of the box, we entwined the base with delicate smilax vines. To the guests at this dinner party, the flowers—white Casablanca lilies and champagne roses—were magnified to look almost twice their normal size.

Around the room, which had traditional columns and moldings, we used lightboxes again—this time to focus on four-foot-high glass urns filled with eight-foot-high branches of deep pink quince. (The vases rested on sixteen-inch-square lightboxes, each holding four seventy-five-watt bulbs. The boxes, in turn, rested on thirty-inch-high round cocktail tables.) In the middle of December, we wanted to bring an unfamiliar flower, like quince, to Texas. The lighting emphasized the naturally graceful lines of the quince branches and made the blossoms beautifully spare yet elegant.

Although the flowers were the focal point of this party, we also swagged the columns with bolts of fifty-four-inch-wide fabric in intense shades of pink, lavender, blue, and yellow. The great lengths of fabric made the traditional room look more contemporary. The fabric swooped from one column to another, cascading down walls. It also changed color. We wrapped a pink cloth around the top of a column but attached a strip of lavender fabric, so that

ABOVE: Huge glass urns filled with quince branches are uplit to dramatize and exaggerate their natural form.

RIGHT: White Casablanca lilies submerged in a round bowl filled to the brim with water appear larger than life. To make the flowers appear larger still, light them from below.

halfway down the column the fabric suddenly became lavender—but the fabric seam remained hidden. To complete the drama, we aimed spotlights through the bolts of fabric to create pools of pink, lavender, yellow, or blue on the ceiling, in the middle of a column, or just above the guests' heads.

LEFT: Low centerpieces call for spotlit bolts of brightly colored fabric to fill the overhead space.

RIGHT: The spotlit fabrics and uplit centerpieces are reflected in the mirrors on the walls. Reflected images seem to double the amount of light and enlarge the space.

ABOVE: The ceiling, normally a blank space, becomes another surface for design when it is covered with colored projections of trees and branches.

LEFT: Four spotlights built into a black pedestal illuminate the quince blossoms.

RIGHT: The light from the centerpiece accentuates the brilliant colors of the napkins and tablecloths.

A Christmas Fantasy Dinner

■ ■ ■ ■ ■ ■ ■ ■ ■ ■ ■ ■ ■ ■ ■ ■ ■

For this winter party at Rockefeller Center in New York City, we took our design idea from the existing decor. We lit the Sea Grill, the restaurant where the party was held, in the same way the Center itself was lit—with hundreds of tiny white Christmas tree lights. The idea of creating a winter-white party, using the sparkle of clear lights, can be applied to any winter party, whether it's a dinner party for four or, as here, a party for 130. The trick is to sustain the white decor of the room—in table, chairs, and lighting—and vary the textures.

At Christmas the focal point of Rockefeller Center is an eighty-foot-high tree decorated with thousands of multi-colored lights. The rest of the Center, however, is lit with white Christmas tree lights. Strands of these lights wrap around the railing that encircles the skating rink, and more lights frame the doorways of the restaurants and buildings in the Center. The gilded statue of Prometheus is surrounded by fir trees lit by white lights.

Inside the Sea Grill, the crossbeams were already lit by tiny lights, and we added yet more lights. We covered the brass light fixtures on the ceiling with blue spruce boughs (artificial because of the danger of fire) into which we tucked sparkling white lights. On the brass sconces, we hung cascading strings of more tiny white lights.

The tables were covered with white cotton cloths woven with sparkly silver threads. For the centerpieces we designed irregularly shaped mounds of artificial snow and buried tiny white lights underneath so that the snow glowed. For fragrance and delicate texture we added white narcissus blossoms, their stems tucked into vials of water. The flowers looked as if they were just poking their heads out of the snow at the first sign of spring.

As a counterpoint to the thousands of white lights in the room, each table had three white candles that were eighteen, twenty-four, and thirty inches high. The candles were large so that they would be noticed and not be lost in the twinkle of the surrounding lights. In addition, the

LEFT: Glamour is created in this below-street-level restaurant solely by the use of lighting. The Sea Grill looks out on two famous New York landmarks: an ice-skating rink and the Christmas tree that towers above it.

ABOVE: At the entrance to the restaurant, curly willow, delphinium, and calla lilies welcome the guests.

■ ■ ■ ■ ■ ■ ■ ■ ■

flicker from the candlelight was a nice contrast to the constant light from the bulbs.

To sustain the winter-white color theme, the white wooden chairs had white moiré cushions. The plates and napkins were white, as was the piano placed in the center of the room.

A note of color was saved for the end of the party, moments after dessert was served. To Billy Roy's piano accompaniment, Julie Wilson sang songs by Noël Coward, George Gershwin, and Cole Porter. She wore a white gardenia in her hair—and, as she stood in an arc of light, her red-sequined dress sparkled.

FAR LEFT, ABOVE: Outside the window, the lights of the Christmas tree twinkle through the glass; inside, tiny white Christmas lights buried under fake snow cast a mysterious golden glow.

FAR LEFT, MIDDLE: Narcissus, lined up in clear glass containers, wait to be cut and arranged.

FAR LEFT, BELOW: Narcissus bloom in a bed of "snow," underlit by battery-operated white lights.

ABOVE LEFT: At this party, light, the most important design element, is both ornament and illumination.

RIGHT: Clear glass balls nestled in the "snow" reflect light from the tree, the candles, and the lights below.

FOLLOWING PAGES: Almost all the surfaces at this party reflect light—the windows, the glittering fake snow, the tableware, the vases, the chairs, the piano, and, especially, the skating rink.

Electronic Birthday

■ ■ ■ ■ ■ ■ ■ ■ ■ ■ ■ ■ ■ ■ ■ ■ ■

Some parties are most successful when they are built around tradition. Everyone expects Christmas trees on Christmas Eve, birthday cakes and candles on birthdays, pumpkins on Halloween. To be too avant-garde can sometimes only disappoint. To give a new twist to an old-fashioned birthday party, we provided the classic elements—party hats, unfurling striped paper noise-makers, helium-filled balloons—but made the lighting different.

Abandoning candles, we lit each of the four tables with a six-foot-long red, blue, green, or yellow plastic tube threaded with a string of lights that, because they were attached to a transformer, looked as if they were moving from one end to the other. The light was animated, and the pools of color cast by the lights on the center of the table changed subtly through the night. Yet these tiny electrical bulbs created a light that was as soft and gentle as candlelight.

The colored light tubes also solved a built-in lighting problem. The dining room has a lovely chandelier that is a perfect lighting fixture over one dinner table set for six or eight. For a party of forty, however, the candles in the chandelier do not cast enough light and leave the corners of the room dark. Guests seated in the center are bathed by the candlelight from above, while those in the corners squirm in semidarkness. The tubes made the lighting equitable. (We hid the electrical cord by making a hole in the tablecloth and running the cord under the cloth and down to the floor.)

Above the guests, four hundred white balloons, interspersed with twelve larger balloons—four red, four yellow, and four blue—floated against the ceiling. Each helium-filled balloon was tied with narrow curling ribbon in white, red, yellow, or green. To keep the eye entertained, some ribbons were three feet in length, others five.

ABOVE: Each table at this unusual birthday party is covered with a white cloth scattered with paper dots that are the same color as the light tube. Guests know where to sit by the color of the polka dots on their escort cards.

TOP: The actual ceiling is lost behind masses of balloons.

LEFT: White balloons and an occasional colored balloon cover the ceiling and reflect light from the centerpieces below. The tube lights in the centerpieces can be made to chase at whatever speed the hostess wants. They flicker electrically, as candles do naturally. Because these moving lights are rarely used, they can rivet the guests' attention.

■ ■ ■ ■ ■ ■ ■ ■ ■ ■

The bright primary colors of the tube lights were repeated in the placecards and in the table design. When the guests picked up their placecards, they discovered another small break with tradition. There were no numbers on the cards that told them which table to sit at—one, two, three, or four. Instead, each card had either red, green, blue, or yellow polka-dot stickers on it. A person who picked up a card with red dots knew he was to sit at the table with the red tube, and a guest with the green polka-dot card headed to the table swimming in a green light. But just in case a guest couldn't figure that out, we also scattered the larger polka dots on the white cotton tablecloths. The polka dots were traffic signs for the guests—and also added a festive note to the tables.

Although candles were absent, flowers were not. We placed white Casablanca lilies in three vases and then single lilies in tiny bud vases. The natural flowers, with their spicy scent, contrasted with the synthetic tubes of light.

LEFT: Blinking lights from the green tube shine on the edges of silver service plates. The colored plastic tubes, filled with strings of white lights, are generally available at theatrical supply shops.

ABOVE RIGHT: Light glows through beakers of lilies.

RIGHT: The bright colors of the tubes and polka dots are repeated on the placecard lettering.

A Golden Performance

For a party on the Promenade at the New York State Theater celebrating the New York City Ballet's performance of Peter Martins's "The Sleeping Beauty," guests entered a four-story space that seemed washed with gold.

Enormous candelabra shirred in gold gauze soared nine feet above the tops of the tables. From each candelabrum rose twelve-inch-high pillar candles, three on the top tier, six on the bottom. Five pillar candles sat on the table tops. The presence of electricity, despite the uplights covered in amber gels, was not detected. The room appeared to be entirely lit by candlelight.

From each arm of the candelabra, we looped a chain of gold or crystal beads. At the bottom of each arm, we suspended a crystal prism, whose faceted edges reflected light.

The height of the candelabra contrasted with the tiniest white flowers—lilies of the valley—nestled in gilded terra-cotta pots. The little pots of delicately scented flowers became small focal points on the tables.

White faille overcloths, printed with white-on-white fleur de lys, covered the tables, while the undercloths were platinum-gray satin. We gathered the top cloth in ten places, and where the cloth was swagged we tied a gold ribbon in a bow, and ran the ribbon to the center of the table. Each place setting looked like a wedge of pie trimmed with gold ribbon, and the spoke design led the eye to the center of the table—the lilies and the candles. The gold chairs had seat covers of the same platinum-gray satin that covered the table.

Throughout the room, the golden, flickering light was reflected over and over again—in the gauze, the chains of gold or crystal beads that were looped from one arm of the candelabra to another, the crystal prisms, the vermeil, the gold ribbons. Finally, the light bounced off the metal chain curtain that covers the entire length of one wall of the Promenade.

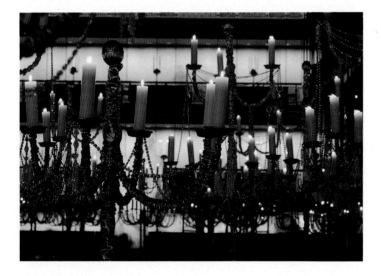

LEFT: Shirred in gold gauze, entwined with gold and crystal beads, the twelve-foot-high candelabra cast flickering, evanescent golden light throughout the Promenade at the New York State Theater.

RIGHT: More than seven hundred pillar candles, placed at three different heights throughout the room, filled the space with tiny, sparkling dots of light.

LEFT: The room, viewed through a forest of golden candelabra.

ABOVE: The delicate lily of the valley centerpieces, tucked into gilded terra-cotta pots, became a focal point because of the green leaves standing out against the white-and-gold table. The plant's soft fragrance is also a sensory lure.

Down-Home Dinner

■ ■ ■ ■ ■ ■ ■ ■ ■ ■ ■ ■ ■ ■ ■

For a dinner party in an eighteenth-century stone house in Bucks County, Pennsylvania, we lit the dining room exactly as Stanley Kubrick lit the dining sequence in his film *Barry Lyndon*—with candlelight. Additional lighting was also provided by massive pine logs burning in the stone fireplace. The soft, flickering firelight cast a lovely amber glow on the dark wood beams and table and the white walls, and made the silver goblets look golden. Except for the four pink uplights in the corners of the room, the room was lit as it might have been in 1723, the year the house was built.

Because the dining room was large and not very bright even during the day, we used masses of white candles ranging from slender tapers to fat, squat pillars. There were candles on the tin chandelier above the table, directly on the table, in sconces above the fireplace, on the mantel, and on the sideboards. Since the candles were at different heights, they lit the table, the ceiling, the walls, and the floor. A beautifully detailed, hand-hooked rug, a colorful Majolica collection on the sideboard, and a wood platter in the shape of a pig were all illuminated. The rug pattern, which included a brown horse and a white gazebo, was clearly visible, as were the muted shades of yellow, rust, turquoise, and green of the Majolica plates and pitchers. To make the eighty-four-inch round table look intimate and inviting to the eight guests at this dinner party, we chose oversized white plates thirteen inches in diameter. On the plates, we laid heavy deep pink Indian napkins, which were sixteen inches square—big and bold to match the scale of the plates.

Phlox and hibiscus arrangements on the table added a further homey touch. The phlox, gathered from the garden outside the dining room door, were deep pink—matching the napkins—pale pink, and white. We tucked their stems into two ten-inch- and two twelve-inch-high flasks, which made the flowers seem to hover in the air.

ABOVE: Except for electric uplights placed in the four corners of this eighteenth-century room, all the lighting comes from candles. Placing uplights in the corners of a room visually expands the space, since each light illuminates two walls and a portion of the ceiling.

RIGHT: One of the secrets of good lighting is having sources of illumination at different heights. Here, candles light the ceiling, walls, mantelpiece, table, and floor.

In stark contrast to the phlox, the stems of the hibiscus were cut short. Placed in white ceramic ramekins two inches high and nestled by each plate, the hibiscus seemed to be floating in a dark pool of water (the table). We used two kinds of silver goblets—one round with a smooth surface and the other cone-shaped with a hammered finish—and each reflected the candlelight differently.

Fête de Famille

■ ■ ■ ■ ■ ■ ■ ■ ■ ■ ■ ■ ■ ■ ■ ■

For a party to benefit AIDS research that was held at Mortimer's restaurant on Manhattan's Upper East Side, we wanted to keep the design light and bright. Hope, not doom, was the keynote. To make the party for seven hundred guests merry, we used sparkling lighting and fabric in the brilliant colors of autumn.

East Seventy-fifth Street, between Lexington and Third avenues, was closed off to traffic and a 120-foot-long tent (actually six adjoining tents) was erected on the asphalt. The trick was to make the great length of the tent seem inviting, not daunting. We tucked three hundred candles in glass fishbowls, tied them with red and orange ribbons, and suspended them from the tent poles at different heights, from a few inches to a foot above the guests' heads. As far as the eye could see, the flames flickered their glittering light, magnified in the glass bowls.

Just as the tiny candles illuminated the space, swaths of red, orange, and yellow fabric crisscrossed and defined the space. The fabric, fifty-four inches wide, sailed through the air from the tent poles and wound up gracefully mounded on the tops of the cocktail tables.

RIGHT TOP: Images of autumn leaves are projected onto the sides and pointed ceiling of the tent to give textural interest to the white canvas.

RIGHT BOTTOM: To entice guests into the tent, votive candles, enclosed in glass bowls, sparkle overhead. The space is filled with bolts of fabric, each heightened by its own spotlight, creating different planes of light and color.

BELOW LEFT: Only one flower, the late-summer giant sunflower, is used at this party—but it is used en masse for maximum dramatic effect.

BELOW: Light clearly intensifies color, and the sunflowers, looking even more golden when spotlit, are the focal points at both ends of the long white tent where the party was held.

■ ■ ■ ■ ■ ■ ■ ■ ■ ■

Each of the six tents, which measured twenty by twenty feet, had a spotlight on each corner. A spotlight with a red gel was aimed at a length of red cloth, a spotlight with a yellow gel zeroed in on a yellow streamer.

We attached templates, which were cut to cast the shapes of leafless branches, to theatrical projection spotlights. (Templates are available at theatrical supply houses.) We projected the branches onto the ceiling of the tent to add pattern to the stark white cloth. (Templates are devices that can be used to create flames, fireworks, moving water, and other, almost limitless, graphic effects.)

The only flowers were sunflowers. Two giant urns, filled with bright yellow sunflowers six feet high, flanked the entrance. At the far end of the tent was a matching pair of urns filled with the same golden flowers.

By using different lighting techniques and simple ribbons, we gave the interior of the tents a brilliance of color that equaled the autumn foliage found in nature.

A circular buffet table commands attention at the center of the tent. Huge clusters of green, purple, and red grapes, entwined with natural grapevines, form the centerpiece. On the table are apples, fruit tarts, and cheeses.

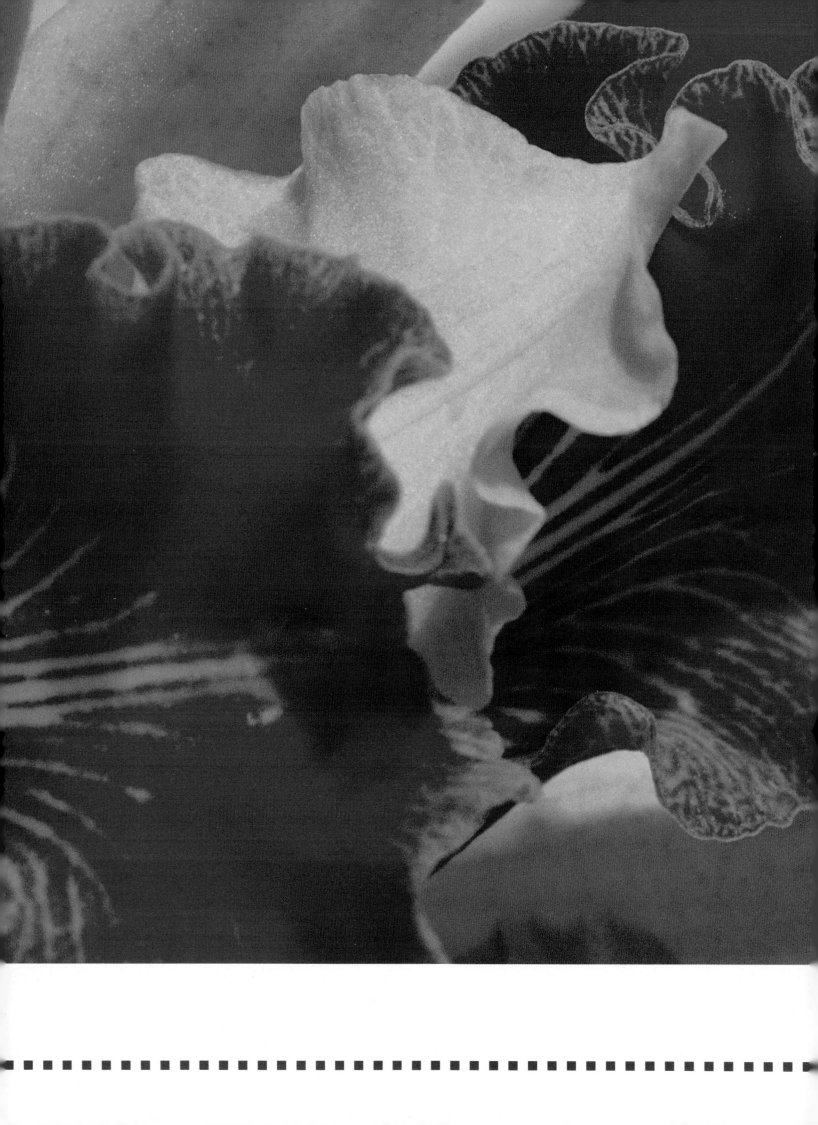

COLOR

Just as lighting evokes mood, color creates energy.

Consider bright colors. Most people are afraid of high-voltage colors, because mixing those colors—red, orange, blue, yellow—might result in garishness. In daily life, most people choose to surround themselves with walls painted white or beige.

At a party, however, people are willing to toss aside their normal inhibitions, such as fear of color. Bright colors make people feel exuberant and perky—instantly. Brilliant colors are a prerequisite for some parties—and inappropriate for others. Can you imagine a beach party without the vivid primary colors of a beach ball? A Chinese wedding demands the color red, the color of good luck. There is no joy in a Mexican fiesta without hot pinks, purples, yellows, and oranges.

In contrast to bright colors, pale colors do not generate the same intensity of feeling. At a formal dinner, for example, we do not want to create a setting that leads to wild abandon. We may want the guests to feel gracious and celebratory but also in self-control. For a memorial service, pale rather than bright colors are appropriate: pale colors signify serenity.

Jewel tones, the colors of gems like emerald, ruby, and sapphire, suggest richness. These colors can be used as tablecloths, but also as streamers and backdrops. They bring a vivid opulence to plain or drab spaces.

■ ■

A monochromatic background—all red, all blue—can make a party highly dramatic and distinctly memorable. People remember the party by the color of the room—or the decor. To create a highly textured monochromatic design, we sometimes take the existing color of a wall and repeat it in the flowers, china, and linen.

The challenge of using color as a major design element is to find the unusual hues, the ones that are hard to describe and are not part of our daily vocabulary, and to mix them. We want to find seven shades of peach that are seen only rarely in flowers—or six shades of blue that exist in the ocean but seldom in flowers.

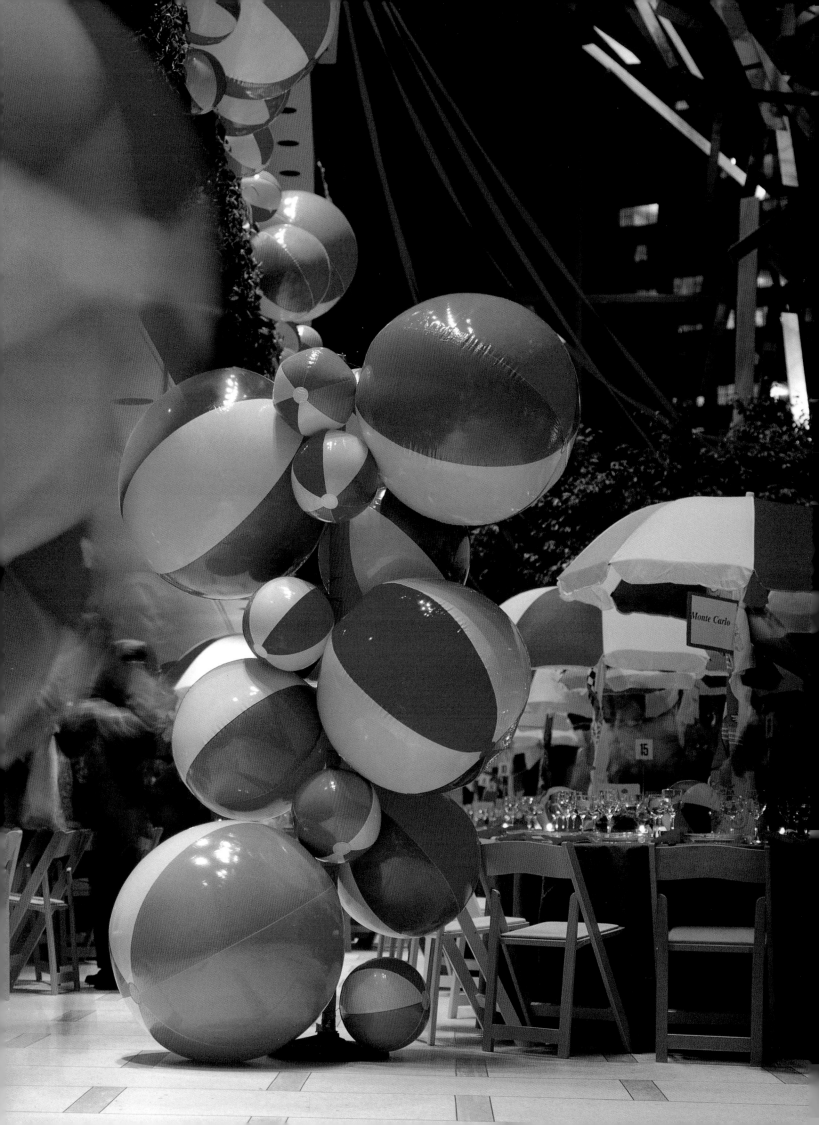

A Beach Party
at Lincoln Center

■ ■ ■ ■ ■ ■ ■ ■ ■ ■ ■ ■ ■ ■ ■ ■ ■ ■

Each year, the Advertising Women of New York hold a party where they screen the winning films from the International Television Commercials Film Festival in Cannes. A dinner party and dancing follow the screening. The women who belong to this professional group are lively and extremely self-confident. They are in a dog-eat-dog business, and when they relax, they know how and when to get rowdy. Shyness is not a professional trait.

For this party, we had the fun of designing the most informal party in the most formal setting. The place was Avery Fisher Hall, a grand concert hall with marble floors and crystal chandeliers at Lincoln Center in Manhattan. Since the film festival was originally held in Cannes, the theme of the party was the beach.

Cocktails preceded the screening. As guests arrived on the loges via the escalator, they saw poles covered with two hundred red, yellow, blue, green, and white beach balls

ABOVE: The red, blue, yellow, green, and white beach umbrellas and strands of ribbons lighten the serious monolithic architecture of Avery Fisher Hall.

FAR LEFT: Beach balls made into totem poles delineate space and fill the overhead area with color.

LEFT: From every angle, tables, chairs, and beach umbrellas provide strong graphic elements.

that ranged in diameter from twelve to forty-eight inches. Beach umbrellas, segmented in the same colors, towered over the tables of hors d'oeuvres. Spotlights cast their beams through the umbrellas into the tables, which were covered in red, blue, green, and yellow cloths. Baskets of food were lined with checked gingham napkins in red or blue and white. The appetizers were as informal as the ambience: bruschetta, pigs-in-blankets, potato chips. But

RIGHT: Ribbons trail from the top balcony to the tops of the umbrellas, and sway with the air currents in the room. Ribbons are yet another easy way to brighten a room—even a small one.

BELOW: Standard rental chairs in bright colors are an inexpensive way to add color to a room.

what made the guests sure to cut loose, even in formal attire, were the lifeguards. Three white lifeguard chairs were perched among the tables of food, and on each chair sat a handsome young man clad only in skimpy swim trunks. This montage of godlike young men and beach balls set the casual tone for the dinner.

After the screening, guests reentered the loges, and saw forty-one patio tables covered with blue, green, purple, turquoise, orange, red, and yellow cloths. Each table was named after a well-known beach, such as Monte Carlo, St. Tropez, and Cap Ferrat. Wrapped around the umbrella pole on each table were fluorescent beach towels, inflatable plastic sharks, and swim fins. There were real portable radios on the tables, and scattered around were the party favors—sunglasses, sea shells, Frisbees, lighted plastic ice cream cones and yo-yos—that guests played with during the party and took home afterward. The only hint of formality was the five votive candles on each table.

LEFT: At every level, from the top balcony to the floor, this room is filled with color. The permanent lighting fixtures of Avery Fisher Hall cast their glow through the beach umbrellas onto the tables, brightening the colors. Below, scantily clad young men pose as lifeguards.

ABOVE: Beach balls, wired together, cascade over the balconies.

LEFT: Battery-operated "ice cream cones" illuminate the center of the tables, which are scattered with sunglasses, swim fins, and beach towels, which, in turn, become party favors.

A Dinner Dance at the Four Seasons

■ ■ ■ ■ ■ ■ ■ ■ ■ ■ ■ ■ ■ ■ ■ ■ ■ ■ ■ ■

For this autumn party at the Four Seasons restaurant in Manhattan, we abandoned the blazing reds, purples, and oranges of fall foliage. Instead, we designed a party using a subtle, subdued autumn palette of salmon, peach, and copper. To make these golden colors stand out, we added a note of contrast—pale blue.

The Four Seasons, designed by the architect Philip Johnson, is an ode to modernism—stark, minimal, formal, and elegant. The architecture is powerful. We added plants, flowers, candles—elements of gaiety that at the same time complemented the architecture.

As guests entered the Grill Room, massive urns filled with spiky pyracantha branches dotted with tiny orange berries greeted them. Small cocktail tables, thirty inches in diameter, were covered with peach linen cloths. Thirty-inch-high beeswax pillars were entwined with smilax vines, white cattleya orchids, and peach begonias. But what gave this room the required dash of glamour were the two hundred votive candles that were placed on the ledge of the balcony.

To go to dinner in the Pool Room, guests had to walk through a very cold, impersonal corridor, where both the walls and floor are marble. To add a visual sense of warmth to the space, we lined the floor with terra-cotta pots filled with peach and orange geraniums.

In the Pool Room, we lit five hundred votive candles around the edge of the square pool. People suddenly noticed what a luxury it was to have a pool in the middle of a metropolitan restaurant.

Four rectangular tables edged the pool. On the outside perimeter, beneath the windows, were twelve round tables. Copper gauze cloths covered all the tables, and the napkins were peach linen. The flowers were salmon amaryllis, champagne roses, flame-orange Mireille roses, peach Doris Ryker roses, and hydrangeas that came in cream, pale blue, pale green, and maroon. In each arrangement were pale-blue grape hyacinths. Although pale

LEFT, TOP: When a party is held in two or more separate rooms, a monochromatic color scheme—shades of peach ranging from pale to deep orange, for example—helps unite the design. In the entrance to the Four Seasons restaurant, branches of orange-berried pyracantha surrounded by orange begonias set the color tone of this party.

LEFT, MIDDLE: Cocktail tables covered in peach taffeta hold centerpieces of thirty-inch-tall cathedral candles entwined with smilax vines, white cattleya orchids, and orange begonia flowers.

LEFT, BOTTOM: Pyracantha, often used in landscape design for the brilliant color of its berries, works well indoors for the same reason.

RIGHT: Peach lilies, pale green hydrangeas, and branches of pyracantha fill garden urns set on classical pedestals, which add a formal note.

blue is not normally associated with autumnal colors, if you look carefully at the leaves you step on during the fall, there are always some—not many, perhaps—that seem to be the color of the sky.

The flowers were the same on all the tables, but the vases were not. Each of the rectangular tables surrounding the pool was fourteen feet long—just long enough for someone to feel alienated. So we designed the flowers (placed in hidden glass bowls) to be low, so that guests could see each other and not feel that they were seated at that awful institution, the dais. On each of the tables, there were three centerpieces, one for every five people. We didn't want people to feel unequal, as if they were subject to a pecking order. (The usual thinking goes like this: The person in the center is clearly the star. The rest are underlings, and the two people at the end are bookends.) To make the long tables friendly, we surrounded the flowers with smilax vines and pillar candles. The smilax trailed down the table, twisting and coiling, interspersed with the peach-colored Doris Ryker roses. The asymmetry of the smilax vines contrasted with the strict formality of the rectangular table.

We matched the contour of the twelve round tables by placing the flowers in thick elliptical glass bowls. Just because the round tables were farther away from the pool didn't necessarily mean that those who sat at them were of lesser importance than those who sat at the rectangular tables flanking the pool—round tables are by nature friendlier and more intimate than long tables.

We also designed the flower arrangements at the round tables to be low because we wanted people to talk. The room, however, has a very high ceiling. To prevent people from feeling overwhelmed by the high ceiling and the bronze chain curtain, we suspended flowers on the wall. Against the chain curtain we hung twenty six-foot-high arrangements of pyracantha branches, hydrangeas, and salmon amaryllis, making the flowers as bold in scale as the architecture.

ABOVE: Five hundred votive candles ring the edge of the pool. An excess of candles can be very dramatic, especially at a dinner party.

LEFT: Warm autumn shades of peach, orange, and copper, found in the flowers, linen, and lighting, fill the Pool Room. The colors are muted, not garish.

RIGHT: Because round tables offer more space in the center than square or rectangular tables, thick, deep elliptical vases can be used to hold flowers.

FAR RIGHT: The ceiling is filled with downlights. At the four corners of the pool, evergreen trees are uplit with peach-tinted spotlights and candles.

BELOW RIGHT: The entire room is ringed with hanging copper bowls filled with salmon amaryllis, cream hydrangeas, and pyracantha branches.

BELOW, FAR RIGHT: Short, thick rolled beeswax candles focus attention on the flowers—and on the faces of the guests. Beeswax candles have a fresh, clean honey scent.

ABOVE: The room is lit by a golden light, created by reflections from candles on the water, the copper tablecloths, and the room's famous chain curtain.

RIGHT: Long tables hold arrangements of monochromatic peach-toned flowers, which are connected to each other by strands of smilax vines.

A Country Brunch

Zinnias, one of summer's most brilliantly colored flowers, were the focal point of a champagne brunch held on a screened porch that overlooked a pond ringed by trees. In the middle of the table was a bouquet of red, yellow, orange, pink, and white zinnias. The colors, especially the yellow, were repeated throughout—in the vase, napkins, tablecloth, and plates.

Flea-market finds can often be transformed into interesting and unusual containers for flowers. Here we used a 1930s metal toy truck painted bright red and yellow. The sides of the truck depicted a farm scene—a boy, a tractor, a cow—that echoed the country theme of the brunch. We lined the truck with black vinyl, which we taped to the sides so that it could hold water for the zinnias.

The tablecloth was white damask crisscrossed in yellow with faggoted edges. The napkins, a vivid yellow, rested on white plates. Surrounding the table were a painted bench, plain dark wood chairs, and hand-painted bar stools with black-and-white holsteins painted on the seats, again echoing the country theme.

In a wicker workbasket, there were more flowers— white tea roses and blue delphinium. The delicacy of these flowers contrasted with the robust zinnias, and added a pale tone to the brilliant reds and yellows in the room.

RIGHT: A verdant green dominates the room in summer.

RIGHT: Bright red and yellow flowers fill a toy truck.

A Fiesta at Lincoln Center

■ ■ ■ ■ ■ ■ ■ ■ ■ ■ ■ ■ ■ ■ ■

A color that is basically soothing is not always festive. Neutral colors like beige or gray, for example, work as serene backdrops to living rooms, offices, or foyers, but alone and unadorned they are not colors that make you want to party. At Lincoln Center in Manhattan, the walls of the Performing Arts Library are beige travertine, a sleek and elegant but understated material. And the space, which is sixty feet by two hundred fifty feet, is austere. We gave the room warmth and interest by using vividly colored Mexican serapes, piñatas, and paper flowers in our design.

The cotton serapes were striped in different combinations of green, yellow, turquoise, cobalt, orange, khaki, rust, and purple. From the serapes, we chose the five predominant background colors—orange, green, turquoise, yellow, purple—and made up round tablecloths and napkins. Then we matched them. A turquoise serape topped a turquoise cloth, a serape with an orange background went over an orange cloth. If a serape had a rust or khaki background, we placed it over a cloth with a contrasting color—orange or purple for a khaki serape, yellow for a rust serape.

Napkins, rolled lengthwise, became exclamation points when placed on black plates. The chairs were also black so that they would not detract from the vivid rainbow of colors on the tables.

On each table a thirty-inch-high slender glass vase held blue and purple delphinium, yellow sunflowers, speckled yellow lilies, pale pink Kwanzan cherry blossoms, white dogwood, and red Gloria mundi roses. From the top of the vase, the flowers rose another four feet into the air.

We surrounded the base of each vase with four paper flowers, each eighteen inches in diameter, in purple, pink, orange, turquoise, or yellow—artifice contrasted with nature.

We lit each table with a spotlight attached to the ceiling and aimed at the vase of flowers, and used votive candles to provide uplight.

ABOVE: Colorful napkins are rolled into exclamation points.

LEFT: Each table is covered with a striped serape in different colors. The serapes set the tone for the Mexican theme and provide a nice alternative to an ordinary tablecloth.

Above the dance floor, we hung piñatas in the shape of jalapeño peppers, coyotes, donkeys, cowboy boots, and parrots.

The beige travertine walls of the room disappeared behind black cloth embedded with tiny Italian white Christmas lights, creating the startling effect of a dark room, seemingly lit by stars, in which the tables floated.

■ ■ ■ ■ ■ ■ ■ ■ ■ ■

ABOVE: Tall glass vases hold full sprays of fresh late-spring flowers, while Mexican paper flowers rest on the table.

RIGHT: The walls of this large room are covered in black fabric dotted with little white lights. This creates an illusion of night, so that darkness at the edges of the room contrasts with the brilliant colors on the tables. Seen from above, the table-top becomes a circular, graphic element, with napkins as strong lines of color.

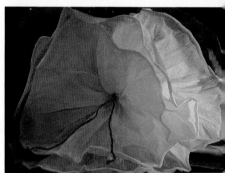

TOP: Sunflowers, delphiniums, and roses are among the flowers on the tables.

ABOVE: Mexican paper flowers are used because of their size and brilliance of color. In the right situation, they are an excellent alternative to real flowers.

FOLLOWING PAGES: Sunflowers represent the exuberance of all late-summer flowers; spotlights intensify the colors in the room.

A Chinese Wedding

For the Chinese, red is the color of good luck and gold the color of wealth. For a traditional Chinese wedding celebration that included an eleven-course banquet, we used these brilliant colors everywhere, from the ceiling to the table to the floor. Red and gold, however, can be used not only for a Chinese wedding but also for a Chinese New Year celebration or just a dinner of Chinese takeout food. The colors are admittedly bright, but can be very dramatic.

The wedding was held at the three-thousand-square-foot Silver Palace restaurant in New York City's China-town. Outside the restaurant, we covered the sidewalk with a red carpet that was twelve feet wide by twenty-four feet long. On the steps leading to the restaurant we placed pots of red begonias and scattered red and pink paper rose petals.

The traditional Chinese dinner is served at a round table that seats ten. Although the waiters serve the guests individual portions of food, they also leave extra food on the platter in the center of the table until that course is finished. Centerpieces were therefore out of the question, so color provided the excitement.

We covered the tables with round tablecloths of bright red satin, in the center of which we hand-painted in gold the Chinese characters for "Double Happiness." When the platters of food were in the middle of the table, they were framed by red and gold, and when the middle was empty, the characters stood out clearly.

Instead of floral centerpieces for the tables we designed individual flower arrangements—one for each guest. These small arrangements added a note of intimacy to the tables and made the guests feel special. Guests could also take the flowers home as a memento of the wedding. For vases we used glass napkin rings into which we tucked the napkins and chopsticks as well as two or three gold, white, pink, or yellow ranunculuses. (The bride's bouquet was made of scarlet, yellow, and peach-colored poppies and ranunculuses.)

We couldn't use candles to light the tables because they would have impeded the waiters, who had to reach into the center of the table to set down the platters of food. So we used the existing lights, dimmed but constant. To distract the guests' attention from the boring lighting—and also to fill the cavernous three-thousand-square-foot space—we suspended eight dozen red-and-gold-silk lanterns, each of which was twenty-four inches in diameter. At this bright, colorful party, even the cake sparkled. It was made in the shape of a pagoda that was frosted in white and gold.

In the entrance to the Chinese restaurant where this wedding reception was held, red ribbons hang from the ceiling and red flowering begonia plants line the steps. Paper rose petals are scattered on the floor—an oft-neglected surface for design.

ABOVE: Clear-glass napkin-ring bud vases hold gold and yellow poppies and ranunculuses, which contrast sharply with the red tablecloths.

LEFT: The wedding cake is in the shape of a pagoda.

To break up the seemingly endless low, flat ceiling of the restaurant, the surface is hung with masses of red and gold Chinese lanterns.

Summer Poolside Lunch

■ ■ ■ ■ ■ ■ ■ ■ ■ ■ ■ ■ ■ ■ ■

Everyone loves to picnic, to eat informally, sitting on a blanket spread on a lawn. But when the picnic is on your own lawn, and there are guests around to help you tote the food and wine from the house to the picnic site, you can dress it up. Plates can be pottery, not paper. Utensils can be sterling silver, not plastic. And you can even place a vase of flowers on the blanket—just as you would if you were indoors.

To set off a picnic against a verdant meadow blooming with yellow heliopsis, yellow coreopsis, and white Queen Anne's lace, we chose brilliant colors from the palette of summer.

For sitting on the grass, we chose an Indian cloth striped in blue, yellow, green, orange, teal, black, and white. There were also matching, deeply fringed napkins.

We dressed up the picnic by a careful choice of colors. Yellow was echoed in a bouquet of sunflowers held in a terra-cotta pot, in the sturdy Italian ceramic plates, and in the yellow-and-white-striped terry-cloth towels that spilled out from the picnic basket. Peaches, shading from gold to pink, shared a wooden bowl with cantaloupes. Even the homely bowl of mustard was given a proper dish of blue and white Japanese porcelain.

In food, however, red was the dominant color. There was the red-orange of ripe local tomatoes, the deep reddish-pink of the watermelon, and the pale pink sheen of prosciutto, laid out in translucent sheets on a wood platter. Red wine sparkled in a glass pitcher.

Because all the elements of the picnic—the food, linen, and china—were boldly colored, it was eye-catching even when set against a vast expanse of green lawn and a bright blue sky.

In the height of summer, everything, from the ripe watermelon to the striped beach towel, is chosen for its brilliant color.

Dinner at the Carlyle

■ ■ ■ ■ ■ ■ ■ ■ ■ ■ ■ ■ ■ ■ ■ ■ ■ ■ ■

At the Carlyle Hotel in Manhattan, when the walls of a room are covered from floor to ceiling in gold paper, the design motif has announced itself. This was a party that had to glow in a golden light. Highlighting the gold were shots of pink and coral in the color of the curtains, the roses in the carpet, and the roses on the fabric covering the seat covers. The color theme, gold and coral, was a given. The trick was to create variations on this theme and make the colors seductive.

Just as the room was papered in gold, with a Japanese motif of mountains, cranes, and apple blossoms, we draped the tables in gold cloths. The tables were surrounded with gilt-edged white wood chairs with lyre-shaped backs and were set with white china banded in a rose and gold filigree, with a center motif of painted pink, lavender, and white blossoms. To make the room even more golden, we set the tables with tall tapers and low beeswax candles. Recessed lighting reflected off the gold paper and cloths, and cast an amber glow around the room.

For the centerpieces, we chose three flowers, each completely different in shape and texture—voluptuous garden roses, delicate sweet peas, and pointed lupine—gathered in dozens of colors that shaded from white to deepest coral, with many subtle variations of peach and pink. There were no two flowers exactly the same color.

When guests entered the room, they were enveloped in a fragrant ambience, where the soft shades of pink set against a golden background were both warm and gentle.

LEFT: The gold tablecloth at this small family celebration repeats the gold of the Chinese wallpaper, the gold-edged china, and the gilt party chairs.

RIGHT, TOP TO BOTTOM: Roses, sweet peas, and phlox are among the flowers in the centerpieces. Although the tables hold the same mixture of flowers in subtle shades of peach, pink, and palest mauve, each arrangement varies slightly. Purple lupine add contrasting color, shape, and texture to the fragile arrangements.

A Memorial Tribute

When a loved one dies, whether it's a spouse, companion, parent, or child, part of the grieving process is, for many, a memorial service. Relatives and friends want to gather and recall the person's life, in silence and in words, with music and with flowers. Because a memorial service is a testament to someone's good character, it must be held with a great measure of elegance, warmth, respect, and beauty.

In a memorial service, flowers symbolize life. They can bring a soft and fragile touch to a church like St. Thomas on Fifth Avenue in Manhattan, where the stone architecture is massive. In the rear of the altar at St. Thomas, we placed two bouquets of white lilies, which flanked the cross. The great bouquets, however, were in front of the altar, flanking the podium. The arrangement had a strong, sculptural background, made of curly willow and wild grasses. The flowers were substantial rather than delicate. There were white delphinium and hydrangeas that shaded from pale gray to pink to green.

After the memorial service, there was a reception at the University Club, where friends and relatives gathered to wipe their tears, eat, drink, talk, and even laugh. To the flowers there—more hydrangeas, more curly willow, more delphinium—we added more color. The delphinium were not just white but also pink and deep purple.

When designing an event for a man, whether it's to honor him at a memorial service or celebrate him at a birthday party, we choose flowers that are white or strongly colored. We may mix these flowers with fruit, grasses, or branches. If the flowers are to stand alone, we sometimes place them in a very strong, bold container, like a thick, weighty glass cylinder, or a low Japanese iron bowl. Naturally, we avoid pastel colors in flowers, and delicate shapes in containers.

ABOVE: Neutral beiges, pale pinks, and dusty greens of flowers, leaves, and wild grasses reflect the colors of the stone-and-marble church. In somber moments, like a memorial service, pale flowers are more appropriate than bright ones.

ABOVE: The flowers, flanking the altar, add a warm touch to an architecturally cool space.

LEFT: Huge stems of delphinium dominate this masculine arrangement. Flowers of this quality and size are grown only in Europe.

An Intimate Dinner

Sometimes a room's color scheme is so perfect that the designer's best strategy is simply to enhance those colors. For a dinner party where the dining room was pink and green, we did just that.

In the dining room, pink and green silk taffeta is swagged and pouffed around the windows. On the walls of the room are hand-painted murals depicting mythical men and women, dressed in quasi-Oriental neo-Classical costumes, frolicking among temples and meadows. Each of the four panels is banded in a green vine motif. From the colors of the draperies and the delicate green vines painted on the murals, we found the natural design for this splendid yet intimate dinner party for twelve.

We focused the table design around the hostess's rare antique sterling silver épergne, an elaborate serving dish that is to food what a candelabrum is to light. At this party, we decided to use the épergne as a vase, which is another one of its functions. Into each of the nine vases—one in the center, and eight on branches—we placed flowers that shaded from white to purple, with pink, in various shades, being the predominant color. There were hoya, tiny pink flowers on long, curving stems; trailing white jasmine; white calla lilies with a pink blush; pale pink nerine lilies; and purple anemones and violets. Roses were in varying shades of pink, lavender, and purple. To add texture and, in a literal sense, flavor, we also added trailing bunches of tiny purple champagne grapes and plump strawberries.

To echo the painted vines on the murals, we wrapped string smilax around the stems of the vases and let it trail along the table intertwined with dried purple and pale

The pink tones in the French panels flanking the fireplace of this city apartment are repeated in the flowers running down the center of the table.

green hydrangeas. Here and there, velvety pink camellias nestled in the smilax and contrasted with the fragile papery hydrangeas. The smilax and flowers wound around the sterling silver salt and pepper shakers, as if to bring notice to the condiments, and continued to twist and curve around the table. We filled gold-etched glass finger bowls with water, and, at the last moment, added a pink baby begonia flower to each bowl.

Since guests entered the dining room last—after passing through the hallway and having cocktails in either the living room or library—we designed arrangements for

LEFT: Roses, jasmine, and nerine lilies are juxtaposed with strawberries and champagne grapes. Fruit, with all its textures and colors, is a versatile design element for a centerpiece.

ABOVE: In the center of the table, a nineteenth-century sterling-silver épergne holds silver baskets filled with flowers and fruit. Tropical smilax vines connect the épergne to sterling-silver shells holding yet more flowers. Curiously, most people don't think of using vines, which lend an organic, curvy line to any table, when entertaining at home.

three different spaces. In each room, the flowers played off the existing objects or decor.

In the hallway that leads into both the living room and the library, we placed a large vase of enormous pale pink tulips—two days before the party. The reason? Tulips completely change position each day, and if they were upright and slightly stiff two days before the party, we knew that they would begin to loosen up and become more languid and voluptuous by the day of the party. The tulips were a signal that beckoned the guests to the other two rooms.

In the library, there is a ceramic vase that looks like a stack of books colored red, black, and white. Because the vase is hard and rigid, as are the massing of books in the library shelves, we designed the flowers to look wild and free. Trailing jasmine cascaded from the vase, which held pink roses, tiny purple skimmia, and pink euphorbia.

In the living room, there was a collection of chinoiserie—a picture, a lamp, a bowl. Because the chinoiserie is heavy and weighted, we chose flowers that were delicate—lilies of the valley, little blue muscari (grape hyacinths), and the cyclamen with its thick, velvet leaves.

In contrast to the flower design in the dining room, the arrangements in the hallway, library, and living room were minimal—preludes to the main event.

TOP AND ABOVE: Pale pink scented begonias float in antique gilt fingerbowls. When placed under water, a flower is magnified.

TOP RIGHT: Scent is an intangible yet powerful design element. In the living room, a bowl of lilies of the valley scents the air.

RIGHT: A vase in the form of a book is filled with roses and euphorbia.

LEFT: The focal point of the hallway is a vase of tulips that seems to be stretching out in the most languorous manner. Some flowers, like tulips, look better one or two days after they've been arranged, when they have had time to "relax."

RIGHT: The symmetry of the wall composition is repeated by the placement of a pair of white gloxinia.

Beribboned

■ ■ ■ ■ ■ ■ ■ ■ ■ ■ ■ ■ ■ ■ ■

For a party that had a low budget but high expectations, we used two inexpensive elements—surprise and color.

The party was a benefit performance and dinner for Planned Parenthood and was held at the Vivian Beaumont Theater at Lincoln Center in Manhattan. The guests knew that the show was at the theater, but they had no clue where the dinner was going to be. Their invitations didn't tell them either. After they had applauded the final act, and the black curtain came down, all they saw when they looked around was a bare proscenium and an equally bare lobby. Clearly something was amiss.

Just as guests were beginning to reach for their programs and evening bags and maybe worry about where they were going to eat, we raised the curtain again. At once, the party came into view on the backstage, and everyone broke into wild applause.

A crisscross of pink, purple, orange, turquoise, chartreuse, and yellow ribbons stretched from the lighting fixtures above the stage to each of the fifty-five tables. The same dazzling colors were used for the tablecloths and the napkins, which were wrapped so they looked like spokes. We alternated the colors so that on an orange table, for example, the napkins might be turquoise, chartreuse, pink, and purple. The stage, which had looked black and bleak, was suddenly filled with color.

Spotlights shone on the centers of the tables, which were covered with sparkling silver, gold, green, and purple paillettes in which we propped six white cattleya orchids. (The flowers and paillettes hid the staples that fastened the ribbons to each table.) The votive candles flickered in the light, and the satin ribbons gleamed.

From a distance, the ribbons seemed to be in the same shades as the tablecloths. Up close, guests saw that the yellow ribbons ranged from buttercup to lemon, the pinks from pale pink to magenta, and the greens from mint to emerald. The ribbons were also different widths, ranging from one and one-half to four inches.

ABOVE: After the guests saw a stage show, the curtains fell. Moments later, the curtains were raised to reveal an empty but brilliantly lit stage—and the beribboned tables beyond.

TOP: Spotlighting, aimed at the center of the table, zeroes in on the white cattleya orchids and reflects off the paillettes.

LEFT: Multicolored ribbons are spotlit to look like laser beams of light crisscrossing this large, high-ceilinged auditorium. Intersecting ribbons of color are bolder and graphically stronger than ribbons hanging straight down.

LEFT: Ribbons of different colors and widths stretch from the centers of the tables to the lighting fixtures above the stage.

RIGHT: Paillettes of many colors are scattered over the tabletops, where the orchids rest. The multicolored pailletes and orchids perform a double function: They add color to the table and also cover the places where the ribbons are attached.

A Russian Party

■ ■ ■ ■ ■ ■ ■ ■ ■ ■ ■ ■ ■ ■ ■ ■ ■ ■ ■

There are few sights less festive than heating pipes running across a ceiling or unpainted gray concrete walls and floors. These problems—visible plumbing and concrete walls—are found in many places, such as most basements, nearly all loft spaces, and, in this case, the Nahamkin Gallery on Madison Avenue in Manhattan. At the gallery, we designed a party celebrating Russian ballet art—costumes and artifacts from 1830 to 1931. We were not allowed to cover the walls, so to focus attention away from the walls and the pipes and dress up a plain setting, we used richly colored and textured fabrics, medallions, and flowers.

To make the colors complement the exhibit, we borrowed directly from the colors of the costumes—ruby, turquoise, and emerald from the velvet dresses and waistcoats, and gold from the Russian icons. Each of the seven tables was covered by a dark green underskirt and a gold overskirt. Chairs were gold with green velvet cushions. The charger plates and flatware were gold vermeil.

But what guests saw first as they approached the gallery and looked into the windows were scarlet, magenta, pink, and blue banners that were forty inches wide and seventy-five feet long. The banners swooped over the pipes and across the twenty-foot-high ceiling, or tumbled down the side of a column. Each banner, which was made of a stiff iridescent rayon gauze, finally ended in a mound in the middle of a table. The banners announced the tables, just as banners announce theatrical events.

To make sure guests could see each other across the tables, we wired flowers to each banner as it rose from the center of the table. By tying the fabric, we narrowed it and cleared the view across the table.

At this party, even the tiebacks were exotic. We inserted orchids in shades of amethyst, emerald, and ruby into the pieces of fabric.

The centerpieces were Russian antiques surrounded by flowers. Because the antiques, which were from the private

ABOVE: At a piano recital, played in a normally austere gallery setting, an urn of flowers, dramatically lit from above, is so large in scale that no other decoration in that immediate area is necessary.

RIGHT: Jewel-toned fabrics soar from the centers of the tables to the ceiling.

collection of Martha Hyder, a renowned collector and balletomane, were exotic and seldom seen in public, we chose flowers whose textures or combinations were also unusual.

On one table, kings from an antique Russian crèche formed the centerpiece. The figures were perched on a mound of red gauze with red and yellow roses and yellow orchids with red throats scattered in the folds of the gauze. The stem of each flower was tucked into a vial of water hidden by the gauze.

ABOVE LEFT: By tying the fabric at strategic points with bracelets of orchids and ribbons, we enable guests to see each other across the tables. These bracelets also become a focal point in the space above the tables.

ABOVE RIGHT: Turquoise fabric enfolds the base of an antique Russian bishop's miter.

LEFT: Chartreuse and magenta cattleya orchids surround a Russian religious icon and a cathedral candle.

RIGHT: Antique Russian dolls stand among voluptuous folds of fabric on the tables.

LEFT: Each table is decorated with different flowers. Here, red roses mingle with gardenias.

ABOVE: A perfect full-blown red rose appears against a pristine background of white cattleya orchids with purple throats.

ABOVE RIGHT: The golden yellow roses are chosen for their depth of color.

RIGHT: Anemones are naturally jewel-toned.

In Shades of Blue

At this lunch for two, set in a foyer, everything from the hand-blown glass window to the wall to the glass plates was a different shade of blue. Some of the blues were deeply colored and sparkling; others were pale and matte. To make a monochromatic color scheme interesting, differing shades must be chosen carefully.

We took the sea theme for this lunch from the color of the wall, which is a "seafoam" blue-green, the color of a lake seen from a distance. The window had panes of pale blue, yellow, lavender, and amber glass, so the light penetrating the foyer was subtle and diffused. To contrast with the muted natural light, we added the sparkle of cobalt-blue glass bowls and a fishbowl suspended in a Victorian wrought-iron stand. The goldfish animated the table, and the blue gravel glittered like tiny faceted blue stones. Two large fake stones, one clear, the other pink, also gleamed in the fishbowl, slightly hidden beneath the gravel.

To contrast with these shiny blues, we used Hermes cotton placemats with a blue and green fireworks motif, and the antique service plates of blue and white china were family heirlooms.

For further contrast and to echo the sea theme, we added natural mother-of-pearl plates and knives, which were from Indonesia, and a seashell. And in a Japanese bronze vase designed in the shape of a fish we arranged bright yellow calla lilies.

ABOVE: Pale yellow calla lilies provide a counterpoint to an all-blue setting.

RIGHT: Even the light, pouring through a tinted-glass window, has a blue cast.

TEXTURE

One of the many joys of entertaining at home is that you can create an ambience so sensual and personal that you envelop your guests in a wealth of texture—the walls, floors, and even ceilings can have many different textures and can be a lot warmer than in a restaurant or a ballroom. The home is where you reveal your largesse and pull out all the stops, whether it's offering rare wines that you have hoarded in your wine cellar or setting the table with Great-grandma Ida's lace-edged handkerchiefs. In your home, you can design a party where everything the guests touch, from the silk-covered seat cushion to the Mexican glasses, is special—not necessarily because it's expensive, but because it reflects your personal taste and feels good.

We create parties that are rich in texture from the floor to ceiling, from the table to the mantelpiece. Wherever the eye turns a candle glows, a mirror sparkles, flowers perfume the room. First, we pull out every new and old accessory we can find—linen, candlesticks, china, stemware, and flatware. Then we mix them for color and texture. We used this approach at two different parties, one in a nineteenth-century barn in Pennsylvania, the other in a Mediterranean-style villa in New York City. The stemware may be delicate and fragile, the plates rustic and

sturdy, the napkins lacy; wines may be poured from elaborate cut-glass decanters or plain silver pitchers.

When we design flowers we always create subtle, rich, and often contrasting textures. We mix soft, small flowers such as sweet peas with larger, more voluptuous flowers such as peonies. The leafy tendrils of a smilax vine contrast with fat, bulbous viburnum. At a party in the New York Public Library, we contrasted the round form of lilac with the very spiky eremurus.

Texture also includes sound, motion, and fragrance. If there is a bubbling fountain or brook nearby, we may site the party near the sound of the moving waters. If there are birds chirping in a cage or fish swimming in a bowl we may want to hear and see the activity. At a party in a New York townhouse, guests sat at a table covered with a copper cloth while they listened to the sounds of water tumbling in an Italian stone fountain. Occasionally the party was punctuated by the sound of birds tweeting. If a room is musty (or even if it isn't) we may want to fill it with especially aromatic flowers, such as gardenias, jasmine, or Casablanca lilies.

■ ■

It is easier to create an all-encompassing rich texture in a home than in an institutional setting. At a concert hall or a ballroom, the flowers, lighting, and architecture may be splendidly theatrical, provocative, and startling. But when you have a party for seven hundred, you would have a hard time finding seven hundred nineteenth-century handmade lace-edged napkins or seven hundred matching antique hand-blown glasses. At the fanciest parties held in institutional settings the china is good but not rare, the stemware is designed for abuse. Only in the home can you entertain in the most extravagant fashion, down to the most intimate detail. In response to such comfort your guests relax in a way that people don't always do in an institutional setting. They are candid and carefree.

Contrast of textures is as essential to a party design as it is to food. A chef would never present a meal that had only soft ingredients—mashed potatoes, mashed turnips, and a mousse. When you look at a table setting, it's the contrast of fragile flowers, crisp linen, and sparkling stemware that makes the table sensuous.

Autumn Still Life

■ ■ ■ ■ ■ ■ ■ ■ ■ ■ ■ ■ ■ ■ ■

For the centerpieces at a wedding reception at the Carlyle Hotel in Manhattan we reinvented an eighteenth-century northern European still-life painting. We took the essential icons—fruits, vegetables, and flowers—but instead of placing them on a wooden table we used birch topiaries.

Like a still-life painting, each topiary was a study in texture and reflected the deep rich colors of autumn. There were ripe yellow Bartlett pears, gleaming Red Delicious apples, dusky green miniature artichokes, full-blown garden roses in pink and deep red, garnet-colored celosia (also known as cockscomb), and bittersweet, with its bright orange berries.

The topiaries were placed in gray Italian stone pots that had a raised-garland motif. The tablecloths had burgundy cabbage roses, pink hydrangeas, and green vines printed on a natural linen background.

ABOVE: Apples and roses, pears and bittersweet, artichokes and hydrangeas compose a topiary created in late autumn.

LEFT: Topiary centerpieces, which do not obstruct the guests' view, are vivid, highly textured focal points.

RIGHT: The topiaries perch on thick birch trunks, which are set in Italian stone pots.

Dinner in a Barn

■ ■ ■ ■ ■ ■ ■ ■ ■ ■ ■ ■ ■ ■ ■ ■ ■

The owner of this rustic nineteenth-century home, a converted barn in Bucks County, Pennsylvania, has no fear of the eclectic. Dark oak beams cross the white-painted ceiling, sisal mats cover the hardwood floors, and the house is filled with an exotic collection of china and textiles. In keeping with this diversity, we wanted to vary the texture of the flowers for this dinner party.

Down the center of the table were five terra-cotta pots, each filled with a different flowering plant—pink dianthus, which look like baby carnations; fluffy lavender trachelium, which resemble oversized dandelions; pale purple pentas, a California species of lavender; yellow alamanda, which has buttery, voluptuous blossoms; and tiny, delicate purple calamint. The perfumes of the flowers did not clash, and the eye was beguiled by the contrasting shapes, colors, and textures.

The most intensely fragrant flower was the four-foot-high flowering rosemary, which we placed on the floor next to the sideboard. It was far enough away from the food so that its scent didn't dominate, and yet, if you bent over the plant you could smell the unmistakable fragrance. Just below one of the long twisting branches of the rosemary we placed a pot of bright pink impatiens.

On the table some of the objects were rough-hewn, while others were fragile. The plates and shallow bowls were chunky cream-colored German pottery hand-painted with tiny blue flowers. Beneath the dishes were woven straw place mats from Africa, with concentric circles in natural, rust, and carnelian. The fine cotton paisley napkins—each one with a different background—were made in the south of France. The napkins were tucked into wood napkin rings hand-carved in Africa in the shapes of tigers, lions, leopards, and camels.

Although the dishes and mats were sturdy, the antique etched crystal glasses, heirlooms from the hostess's grandmother, were extremely fragile. Banded in gold leaf, each glass held a votive candle in an inch of water. (The water prevents the candle from burning too low and cracking the glass, and also makes removing the candle easier.) In contrast to the glasses, which functioned as upscale hurricane lamps, there were also antique iron candlesticks decorated with a leaf motif. Since the dining area is not wired for electricity, we also lit the twelve candles on the iron candelabrum overhead. On the sideboard we scattered more of Grandma's glasses, each holding a candle.

Food was served from terra-cotta casseroles on the sideboard. To draw attention to the food, we placed a pot of spotted white begonia hovering over the casserole.

What the table revealed was the strong personality of the hostess, who prefers the strength of rustic, sometimes primitive fabrics and pottery—but who can mix them with sophisticated and opulent crystal to create a lavish yet appropriate tone for a dinner in a country house.

Sisal carpeting, rough-wood walls, terra-cotta pots, flowering plants, and gold-etched crystal are some of the many textures at this party.

■ ■ ■ ■ ■ ■ ■ ■ ■ ■

A Summer Dinner at the New York Public Library

■ ■ ■ ■ ■ ■ ■ ■ ■ ■ ■ ■ ■ ■ ■ ■

For a summer party at the Celeste Bartos Forum of the New York Public Library, we brought the outdoors inside. As guests walked through the ten-foot-tall brass doors, they saw vases filled with lavender delphinium, white dendrobium orchids, pink lilies, purple lilacs—and spiky golden eremurus. The gold of the eremurus was repeated in the faille tablecloths, which in turn matched the color of the marble walls. But what was most pronounced was the scent of lilacs. In each thirty-inch-high vase there were at least ten branches of lilac, which made the room not only look summery, but *smell* of summer.

As the guests entered the library, however, there was no sign that the party would revolve around the scent of lilacs. In the Great Hall, the entrance to the library, we filled a faux terra cotta urn with summer flowers. There were delphinium in four different shades of blue—midnight blue, purple, purple with white centers, and purple with pale blue edges. There were also golden lilies, white dogwood, lavender lilac, and spiky sienna-colored eremurus. Tiny, delicate pink deutzia were also tucked into the arrangement, which soared fifteen feet above the floor.

Downstairs, at the entrance to the Forum, we sustained the classical theme by perching faux stone urns on two columns. The vases were filled with lilacs, burgundy trumpet lilies, white peonies, purple delphinium, lavender scabiosa, white mock orange blossoms, pink deutzia, and sienna eremurus.

Sprays of eremurus shooting up from tall palace vases help fill the vast domed overhead space of this historic building. Stars are projected through a blue wash onto the ceiling.

As guests entered the Forum, they were enveloped by the fragrance of lilacs. In an urban setting this splendid, subtle, never too-sweet scent is refreshing because lilacs in such abundance are unexpected. When fragrance is used as a design element, the flowers must be chosen carefully. In excess, some flowers like gardenias, jasmine, and narcissus can be cloyingly sweet. To some people, rubrum lilies are overwhelmingly spicy. Other flowers, like chrysanthemums, work beautifully in the garden, but when gathered in large bunches have an acrid funereal smell. And when the aroma of the flowers dominates the room, the food served shouldn't have a strong or distinct odor.

LEFT AND ABOVE: The Great Hall, with its marble floors and classic stone columns, is made warmer by the simple presence of flowers.

RIGHT: In the four corners of the Celeste Bartos Forum, large uplit glass urns hold delphinium in many shades of blue.

Dinner in a New York Townhouse

■ ■ ■ ■ ■ ■ ■ ■ ■ ■ ■ ■ ■ ■ ■ ■ ■ ■ ■

This dining room, with its pale gold silk-covered walls, French gilt chairs, and chandelier, is naturally opulent. It is also extremely formal. To make guests feel comfortable in such a setting, our design for a summer dinner mixed formal and informal elements. The result was a room that had an elegant yet cozy look.

The flowers were lush—orange and white poppies, pink French lupine, pink and white columbine—but because they cascaded willy-nilly down the center of the table, the effect was carefree and lighthearted. There were two kinds of trailing vines: flowering pink jasmine and smilax. Beaded fruit (Styrofoam fruit shapes studded with beads)—oranges, lemons, and peaches in orange, yellow, and pink—contrasted with the delicate flowers and vines and reflected the light. We also wound the vines around the candelabra, which held five tapers each, the antique frosted wine decanters, and the four beeswax candles. As guests reached to pour themselves wine, their hands brushed against the flowers and shiny green leaves.

The ecru linen napkins had two-inch lace hems, but we folded them so casually that the merest touch made them flutter open. The napkins, which were heirlooms, were placed on rustic Italian ceramic plates that were hand-painted green and yellow—the same colors as the striped cushions on the chairs. The plates would have been as appropriate in a rustic bungalow as they were in this Manhattan townhouse. The napkins were as formal as the plates were informal.

On the mantelpiece we placed orange poppies, pink and orange lily heads, and pink saponaria, and entwined the flowers with smilax vines and more beaded fruit in even bolder colors—pink, yellow, green, orange, and red. The beaded fruit caught the light cast by the candles, which were enclosed in nineteenth-century etched-glass hurricane lamps. In the mirror above the mantelpiece, the candlelight was also reflected. Leafy tendrils cascaded over the mantelpiece, adding a delicate tracery to the wood.

A contrast of textures: silk-covered walls and chairs, iron chandelier and candelabra, and a highly polished mahogany table.

LEFT: The centerpiece juxtaposes poppies with fragile columbine, pointy lupine, and sparkling beaded fruit. The fruit, although artificial, adds solidity to the design, and sustains the nature motif.

RIGHT: The sheer, tissuepaper quality of the poppy plays off against the hard yet glittering surface of the beaded fruit.

A Glowing Copper Party

Some rooms offer more intriguing architectural details—or texture, if you will—than others. One room may have a fireplace, another may face a garden. In designing this dinner party, we chose to set up the dinner in a room that looked onto a skylit courtyard filled with birds, flowers, and a fountain. We wanted to challenge four of the senses—sight, hearing, smell, and touch (taste was left to the caterer)—and cosset the guests in a rich panoply of texture.

The colors were a warm, burnished coppery gold and white. The table was covered in a dark copper lamé cloth that gave off a metallic gleam in the candlelight but was soft and silky to the touch. The vermeil plates and flatware added the warmth of gold to the table. Even the rusted iron stand, which was garlanded with leaves and held the centerpiece, added another metallic texture to the table.

In contrast to the copper and gold, the flowers were a pristine, cool white—plump peonies with pink-tinged petals and a light grassy scent, and viburnum, which shaded to the palest green. Napkins were white linen, and the candles were beeswax. Iridescent hand-blown glasses gave another texture to the table: the top of each glass was lightly frosted, while the rest of the glass was smooth. To contrast with these slender glasses, there were also over-sized balloon goblets.

The skylit courtyard adjacent to the dining room was filled with eight-foot-high bamboo trees. A staghorn fern cascaded down a wall. On a stone table sat pots of ochre, chartreuse, and white orchids. On the stone floor were yet more terra-cotta pots, some filled with white daisies, others with white Casablanca lilies. Ivy was also abundant.

Finally, there were the sounds. Water bubbled from a stone fountain the host had brought back from Capri four years earlier. And two talkative green parakeets chirped in a three-tiered bamboo birdcage.

ABOVE: Peonies are chosen for their lush and overripe look.

LEFT: Fabric, chinaware, and flatware with reflective qualities contrast with soft, light-absorbing peonies. The warm, shimmering copper gauze tablecloth shares its metallic sheen with the vermeil flatware and plates.

Post-Wedding Celebration at Home

By its location and design, this dining room is inherently glamorous. First, the room overlooks Central Park, with its changing leaves, reservoir, and grassy meadows. Second, from floor to ceiling the white walls are paneled in beveled mirrors so that the room, even when empty, literally sparkles day and night.

For a party for thirty celebrating a recent wedding, we sustained the pristine silver and white decor, but made it complex and intriguing by combining many textures. Only the flowers and a Monet painting hanging on the mirrored wall added color.

We began with a white background. We set the tables with the hostess's white-on-white organdy cloths appliquéd in linen. The white linen napkins, each embroidered with the hostess's monogram, also had double textures.

Even the chairs were sensual. Painted in matte silver, they were designed after nineteenth-century French ballroom chairs and have substantial wood frames that are at least an inch thicker than those found on most party or ballroom chairs. When you place a hand on the back of one of these chairs, you feel a beautifully curved piece of wood with a smooth patina that is warm to the touch. The seat cushions were upholstered a silvery-beige silk satin, which sparkled with light.

Each table setting was ornate and voluptuous. The vases for the centerpieces, the flatware, the wine goblets, and the tiny flower pots engraved with each guest's monogram (which doubled as party favors) were all sterling silver. The ornate silver vases and the candlesticks dated from the eighteenth century; the simple miniature pots were new.

LEFT: A door is not just an entrance to a room—it is also a picture frame. Here, a perfectly proportioned door frames a tall centerpiece.

RIGHT: A Monet painting competes with the centerpiece for the guests' attention.

LEFT: Bright melon peonies and viburnum balls stand out against an almost colorless background.

ABOVE: A silver flower pot filled with a tiny arrangement of white lilacs is engraved with a guest's initials.

ABOVE RIGHT AND BELOW: The sterling-silver pots, each of which holds a different arrangement, are party favors.

FAR RIGHT: Even the white-on-white organdy cloth, which was appliquéd in linen, was chosen for its variations in texture. In the style of the White House, a placecard rests in the center of a simply folded napkin, instead of on the table.

For the cool, shimmering silver vases for the centerpieces we designed classical bouquets. The center table had coral peonies, purple fritillaria, and pale green viburnum. The side tables had smaller centerpieces of coral and pink peonies, viburnum, white columbine, and lavender sweet peas. In contrast to the brilliantly colored formal centerpieces, each little flower pot was filled with an informal arrangement of paler flowers—grape hyacinths, lilacs, phlox, and sweet peas. Each of the tiny bouquets was different, so guests felt they were singled out for special attention. Candles provided soft light, while spotlights recessed in the ceiling shone on the centerpieces.

LEFT AND ABOVE:
Columbine, in a rare shade of
ivory, is tucked among the
peonies and viburnum.

RIGHT: The silver-leafed
chairs add yet more understated texture. The tables on
either side of the middle table hold shorter centerpieces,
for symmetry.

...PROGRESSION

■ ■

S ome of the most intriguing parties are those that have a progression to them—a beginning, middle, and end—and possibly even a detour or a pause in between. These parties have the same appeal as a mystery novel or a dance contest. They reveal themselves at carefully orchestrated intervals, yet build inevitably to a climax.

The parties in this chapter illustrate different kinds of progression. Some are set indoors, others outdoors, but all take the guests on a journey. At some, cocktails, dinner, and dessert were served separately, but in each room there was a surprise.

As you read this chapter, don't feel you have to duplicate the parties, which are particularly lavish. What you can borrow is the rhythm, the timing, and elements of the design. These parties are designed to be experienced as a Chinese garden is experienced. If you are in one pavilion, you cannot see the next one because either the path curves or trees have been planted to obscure its view. In our parties, we expose just one segment of the party at a time, and keep the rest hidden and secret. As the party progresses, the next segment is revealed. A party can be simple or grand, but it's important to make it progress, to get the guests moving.

The first requirement for a progressive party is a great deal of planning. Unlike an

informal dinner party, where people stand around for cocktails, then simply sit down and eat, a party that progresses demands perfect timing. Cocktails should last an hour at most, and the design of the cocktail space should never be as extravagant as the dinner space. Once cocktails are finished, dinner must begin immediately. Desserts, which may be served in yet another room, must also be offered on time. The timing should be done gracefully, so that the guests are unaware that there is a timetable. As people progress through the party, they do so with anticipation, with hungry stomachs and eyes.

For a Mexican fiesta, there was a progression from a long driveway through a center hall to a rear porch, through the gardens, onto a terrace by the pool, and finally to a pavilion. Every half hour or hour, the vista and ambience changed radically.

For an indoor party in a Manhattan apartment, guests moved from the top-floor foyer to a library, where they had cocktails. For dinner, they went downstairs to the dining room, and then to the living room for entertainment and dessert.

Even as people progress through a party, and the design and ambience shift and change, we maintain a unity of design, whether it's in the colors, flowers, or theme.

A Progressive Fiesta

■ ■ ■ ■ ■ ■ ■ ■ ■ ■ ■ ■ ■ ■ ■ ■

For this party in Locust Valley, Long Island, we combined the casualness of a Mexican party—margaritas, piñatas, and big paper flowers—with the formality of reception cards and a clear path of progression. Each step of the party, from cocktails to dinner, was programmed so that the guests could explore the architecture of the house, the formal gardens, and the landscape, all brilliantly lit by torches.

The party began on the sprawling back porch, where guests were greeted with frosty margaritas made with fresh lime juice. Six parrots with turquoise, green, yellow, and orange plumage sat on branches of the trees, peering at the guests. Some of the parrots wore miniature paper sombreros.

With margaritas in their hands, guests stepped off the porch and, guided by the flames of the garden torches, walked into formal gardens blooming with delphinium, roses, and lupine.

LEFT: Large piñatas and paper flowers set the theme at the entrance to this Mexican party.

RIGHT: Sombreros lavishly embroidered in silver and gold threads, piñatas, paper flowers, and colorful serapes cover a table that holds placecards.

LEFT: Terra-cotta pots, holding flaming garden torches and paper flowers, line the steps leading to the party.

RIGHT: A paper flower and a sombrero adorn the center pole on each table.

On their way to dinner, guests walked down flagstone steps lit by more garden torches. Terra-cotta pots filled with purple, pink, white, green, and yellow paper flowers, fourteen inches in diameter, were placed on every other step. At the foot of the steps was a short path leading to the octagonal poolhouse, where guests found a reception card table covered in three brilliantly colored serapes. The table was canopied by a twelve-foot-tall inverted parasol wrapped in yellow fabric. Attached to the parasol were more serapes, pink and gold paper flowers, and piñatas in the shape of a white steer head, a green cactus, a green chili pepper, and two sombreros—nearly every icon of a Mexican fiesta.

Dinner was set around the pool. Canopies in bright shades of magenta, red, green, and yellow covered the tables. Because the party was outside, we illuminated each canopy with a sixty-watt light bulb, which made the canopy seem to glow from within. From each of the four corners of the canopy we suspended votive candles tucked into fishbowls. On each table piñatas, serapes, and sombreros were wound around the stem of the canopies. Napkins and chairs were pink, red, yellow, orange, and turquoise. Paper flowers, eighteen inches in diameter, were clustered on the table. Yet more votive candles, which sat in terra-cotta pots, illuminated the faces of the guests. Around the pool were fourteen-inch round terra-cotta pots filled with large paper flowers and three-foot-high flaming torches. Styrofoam-based islands covered with large monstera leaves, gardenias, white orchids, candles, and smilax vines drifted on the pool.

After dinner, there was dancing. Disco music blared in the poolhouse, and even the furniture was transformed and covered with serapes.

149

ABOVE: An electric light bulb illuminates the inside of each canopy. The brilliant colors—red, fuchsia, orange, yellow, turquoise—reinforce the Mexican theme.

LEFT: A floating island of monstera leaves and gardenias breaks a table's reflection in the pool.

A Summer Wedding

From dusk to midnight, the moods, the settings—even the lighting—changed at this lavish wedding held on the bride's family's estate in Peapack, New Jersey.

Guests began arriving at sunset, which was the perfect moment for this summer wedding to begin. To reach the house guests had to drive up a winding road past a perfect bucolic scene: horses grazing in a pasture near early-twentieth-century red-brick stables trimmed in white wood. Valets parked the cars, and to the right of the house, the guests could see the white wedding canopy, and behind it a white tent. Then they smelled the exotic scent of gardenias, the first hint that a party was about to begin.

The canopy, which covered the curving brick path leading to the wedding tent, had gardenias and vines of

RIGHT: An antique garden urn filled with eremurus, peonies, and Chinese dogwood sits on a garden wall, hinting at the festivities to come.

BELOW: In the center of each cocktail table, roses, peonies, and sweet peas tumble from a Victorian basket, a perfect container for a centerpiece.

smilax wound around its posts. In the white wedding tent, where a voluptuous formality set the tone, the focal point was the chuppa, the canopy used for Jewish marriage ceremonies. Swagged and pouffed in white satin and gauze, it suggested a royal canopy. Wood poles supported it, and nosegays of white Casablanca lilies and baby's breath entwined the poles. Rows of white wood chairs were set in a curve (to echo the shape of the chuppa) and alternately decorated with nosegays of pale pink roses, sweet peas, and peonies. The center posts were tied with white satin ribbons, which fluttered in the breeze.

After the ceremony, which took place from six-fifteen to six-forty-five, guests left the wedding tent, passed through the receiving line, and entered the formal garden, where for the first time there was a lavish yet subtle use of color—twenty-four-inch round tables covered in pale lavender, yellow, pink, blue, or celadon cloths. The lighthearted colors signaled the beginning of the cocktail hour, which lasted until seven-thirty. At the entrance to the garden a table was set with a classic cast-iron garden urn, which held an enormous, four-foot-high bouquet of peonies,

ABOVE LEFT: At dinner, two-tiered silver candelabra hold champagne roses, white delphinium, pale pink lilies, and cascades of smilax and sweet peas.

ABOVE RIGHT: Around the table, at every other place setting, the tablecloth is gathered and the swag accentuated by a nosegay of gardenias. Even at a formal dinner, napkins are best grasped when folded in a casual, yet neat, triangle.

RIGHT: The double-tier candelabra contrast high and low arrangements of flowers. On the top tier, long-stemmed, four-foot-high stalks of white delphinium and long-stemmed roses stretch to the ceiling. On the lower tier, there are short-stemmed flowers—ranunculuses, sweet peas, and garden roses.

roses, and pink dogwood. On the cocktail tables, wicker baskets tied with metal ribbon bows held peonies, roses, bouvardia, wild sweet pea, and lisianthus.

Even the pool had been decorated. Floating islands of white candles, gardenias, baby's breath, and monstera leaves (large green fronds) drifted across the water. (The flowers and leaves had been set in green Styrofoam.)

At seven-twenty-five the father of the bride walked into the main tent, five minutes before his guests, to have a first peek. He gasped. The tent was an ethereal all-white setting, the only color that of the flowers. Spotlights clamped to the poles shone on the nine-foot-high centerpieces—four-foot-high, double-tiered silver candelabra filled with peonies, champagne roses, pink roses, rubrum lilies, sweet peas, white delphinium, Japanese dogwood, and freesias.

The tables were lit with two kinds of candles—white votives gave uplight while thirty-six-inch-high white tapers added scale to the centerpiece. We covered the tables with white moiré tablecloths and, with a staple gun, gathered the sides of the cloth into poufs. Then the staples were covered with white gardenias tied with white ribbon. White wood chairs surrounded the tables. The white china was banded in cobalt and gold. Columns were wrapped in white fabric, which also crisscrossed the tent from pole to pole, adding drama to the ceiling. Pink uplights were placed around the perimeter of the tent, casting a rosy glow and seemingly enlarging the space.

Finally, there was the wedding cake, which sat on its own table. Sylvia Weinstock, a Manhattan baker, made a cake on which there were cascades of sugar flowers: lavender iris; pale yellow, pink, and cream roses; lilies of the valley; and pink anemones. The sugar flowers matched the colors in the bridesmaids' bouquets. Since the bride and bridesmaids cannot eat their dinner or dance while holding their flowers, we asked them to place their bouquets of pink and white roses and sweet peas around the cake. Nature contrasted with artifice.

Each side of the tent consisted of two layers—one was white cloth, the other transparent plastic. To keep the interior of the tent hidden from outside view, we covered the entrance to the tent with the white cloth. But once the guests were inside, they could see through the transparent sides of the tent and look out onto the green pastures and the rose garden.

When the wedding dinner ended, the guests left the tent and walked down the cobbled brick path, which by midnight was lit by dozens of white candles tucked into hurricane lamps.

ABOVE: Sylvia Weinstock made the cake and sugar flowers to match the colors and species in the bouquets.

LEFT: Individual white delphinium florets with black centers mingle with roses in the bride's bouquet.

LEFT: Roses, purchased as buds, are cared for so that they are in full bloom on the wedding day.

RIGHT, TOP TO BOTTOM: Roses, emblematic of romance, are chosen for their pale pink or peach tones. White roses in buckets wait to be gathered into bouquets. Dutch hybrid lisianthus are among the flowers in the centerpieces. Local garden sweet peas in pink, magenta, and lavender add an informal note to the arrangements in the candelabra.

Roses, Roses, Roses

■■■■■■■■■■■■■■■■■

Built in 1911, the New York Public Library is a Beaux Arts white marble "temple." Inside, there are soaring columns, rotundas, and hand-painted frescoes. The building is palatial, yet the design that we created for a corporate investment banking firm's twentieth-anniversary celebration is one that can easily be reduced in scale and work just as well in a suburban home or in an apartment.

It's always a good idea to let guests know right away that your party is a special occasion. The entrance is the first clue. At this party, for example, the steps to the library's main entrance normally have no canopy. On this night, however, a white one undulated down the staircase. We wanted even the most casual passerby to know that this night was different. In the main entrance hall, the columns were illuminated by pink uplights. We also uplit the ceiling to draw attention to the arches and the balustrades.

In the hall, what caught the eye immediately was the center table, a seventy-two-inch round table draped in brick-colored faille and topped by a three-feet-high stone urn filled with magnolias, curly willow, giant French stock, calla lilies, and pink and white quince. From the floor to the tip of the magnolia branches, the arrangement was fourteen feet high. (This party was held in February; the magnolias were brought up from Maryland and forced to open by placing them in a warm, sunny room.)

On a smaller, sixty-inch round table, the only other decorated table in the foyer, a glass vase held peach-colored

LEFT: Flowers make good "markers" for each stage of a party. Here, a twelve-foot-high arrangement of flowers and branches greets guests as they enter the New York Public Library.

ABOVE RIGHT: In the center of the rotunda, masses of early-summer flowers, including delphinium and tulips, soar from an iron urn.

RIGHT: To draw guests to the placecard table, salmon amaryllis, pink tulips, and viburnum balls are arranged in a glass bowl, which rests in an iron stand ringed with rusted-metal leaves.

ABOVE LEFT: Pink dogwood and viburnum are among the flowers in two gigantic arrangements that flank the door to the room where dinner is served.

LEFT: Roses of many hues—red, pink, yellow, peach, champagne—are ideal for topiary centerpieces and can be combined in infinite ways, so that each centerpiece is different. The bold round shape adds volume above the head level, allowing guests to see across the table.

ABOVE MIDDLE: Gold tassels make standard-issue rental chairs less prosaic.

ABOVE RIGHT: An eagle topiary made of smilax vines, one of a pair flanking the door to the room where dinner is served, forms a kind of living sculpture, adding texture and signaling the start of the "main event."

French tulips, French lilacs, pale green viburnum, and white sweet peas. On this table were the placecards. By the location of the table, near a flight of stairs, the guests knew where to go next.

The McGraw rotunda on the third floor, where cocktails were held, is a magnificent space, with oak-paneled walls and hand-painted frescoes. The ceiling is also forty feet high. Here, the twenty-four-inch round tables were also covered in brick-colored faille. Again, there was a center table with a large flower arrangement that included all the flowers seen downstairs in Astor Hall except for one addition—white tulips. To sustain a design, we often repeat some of the same flowers from room to room, but always add new ones to provide a fresh color, texture, and fragrance. On the little tables, the vases were miniature cast-iron urns, which echoed the large urn seen downstairs. Flowers included purple tulips; red, pink, and lavender anemones; white narcissus; lavender grape hyacinths; and red miniature roses. Cocktails lasted one hour. Hors d'oeuvres were passed.

For dinner, the guests went to the Celeste Bartos Forum, whose entrance was flanked by ten-foot-high flowering quince branches in faux stone urns. On each of the twenty-six tables was a unique round topiary of roses. On each

topiary, the white birch stem was entwined with smilax. The roses were dazzling—cream-colored, velvety burgundy, and tiny, tight red ramblers.

To highlight the flowers, there were spotlights covered with different-colored gels. Peach lights were aimed at topiaries that had predominantly peach or yellow roses. Pink lights shone on red or pink topiaries. Inside the entrance, the doorway was flanked by two smilax topiaries in the shape of birds, which were lit by green gels.

The tables were covered with damask cloths that had a silver design on a pale gray background. The flatware was vermeil, and the beeswax candles were set in hurricane lamps. Cut crystal added an extra sparkle. We chose gold chairs for both the McGraw rotunda and the Forum, and for the dinner, we gave them an extra detail: gold tassels dangling from the back.

Toward the corners of the room were four groups of four classical columns each. To make use of this architectural element, we added to each group a four-foot-high faux stone fifth column, which was used as a pedestal. On it we placed a lightbox, which enclosed four seventy-five-watt spotlights. The lightbox, in turn, supported a four-foot-high glass vase filled with branches of pink and white quince that reached nearly to the ceiling.

LEFT: The greenhouselike architecture of the room is washed with blue light and shot with bright white stars.

BELOW LEFT: Red and yellow roses make an odd but successful arrangement.

RIGHT: Very dramatic lighting makes the room exceptionally romantic, while thousands of roses perfume the space.

Beauty and the Beast

■■■■■■■■■■■■■■■■■■ ■

This party is a story of progression and of enchantment. Each year in Manhattan, several different parties are held at volunteers' homes to raise money for the New York Public Library. Usually the party is designed around a particular book—in this case, *Beauty and the Beast*. Although we borrowed images of Beauty and the Beast from different versions of the story, the party was an homage to, and improvisational reenactment of, the classic film directed by Jean Cocteau starring Josette Day and Jean Marais.

The moment the guests stepped off the elevator in the apartment building, they were enveloped in mist from a fog machine. As they became accustomed to the dim light, they saw through the mist a three-foot-high wood sculpture of a lion, which we called the Beast. Standing next to him was an eight-foot-tall hand-painted portrait of Beauty. Just beyond Beauty and the Beast was an open door covered with white gauze. Behind the gossamer fabric a white, ghostly face stared out with eyes that followed each movement of the guests. (In the film, there are spectral figures whose eyes follow Beauty but whose bodies are never seen.)

In the hostess's library, where the party began, two paintings of Beauty and the Beast, which we had commissioned for the party, covered the windows. Each measured four by eight feet. Black masks edged with shocking-pink feathers were scattered about the room—an invitation to the guests to pick them up, wear them, and enter an ephemeral world of mystery and fantasy. Hors d'oeuvres and cocktails were served by silent, ghostly waiters, whose hair and bodies were painted white. To make the waiters seem even less corporeal, we clothed them in scant white loincloths. The trays of food were decorated with plaster of Paris hands and feet. Now and then we turned on the fog machine, and guests seemed to disappear in the mist. Conversations were suspended.

After forty-five minutes of cocktails, guests were led toward another room, through a second door that was

LEFT: Oversized artists' renditions of illustrations from *Beauty and the Beast* cover the windows at this hostess's elegant apartment. This illustration depicts the only time of the day that Beauty and the Beast regularly met—at dinner.

RIGHT: At cocktails in the library, guests quickly learn the theme of this party.

covered in gauze. Here we reenacted another scene from the film. In the movie, as Beauty's father enters the Beast's castle, arms holding candelabra light the grand hall. The guests saw a white-painted arm slowly waving a candelabrum toward the room where dinner was going to be served.

In the dining room, we swagged sixty-inch-wide bolts of gauze around the windows, the tops of the seven tables, and around a four-foot-high, ten-armed silver candelabrum. Normally we would have arranged flowers in the vases of the candelabrum, but here we put mounds of live moss into which we placed white candles—fat pillar candles in the lower arms and slender tapers in the upper arms. At the base of the candelabrum, we placed more hands and feet made of plaster of Paris. The effect was arresting and unearthly.

In the film, the Beast gives Beauty jewels, including a spectacular pearl necklace. We scattered fake jewels—rubies, diamonds, sapphires, emeralds—around the table. Some stones were loose, others were made up as rings and bracelets. For men, there were gold-colored crowns, and for the women, more masks trimmed in feathers.

Most dinners end with dessert at the table. This one did not. Guests were invited to go to the living room, where

LEFT: Thirty-inch-tall candles extend the height of the candelabra, while pillar candles cast a glow on the casually draped gauze.

BELOW: Candelabra, vintage wine, and gauze cluster in the centers of the tables.

BELOW: On the tops of the dinner tables, costume jewelry, which doubles as party favors, embellishes plaster casts of arms and hands.

Billy Roy, a jazz pianist and accompanist to singer Julie Wilson, played songs from the '20s, '30s, and '40s while tiny desserts were passed. There were miniature Madeleines, raspberry tarts, and persimmon-whiskey pudding served in sake cups. Because the desserts were finger foods, people could eat and listen to the music without having to use knives and forks and create a clatter.

In this room, we made a final flourish of white gauze. We swagged the windows with yards and yards of this sheer fabric. Here, also, we introduced flowers. For drama, we filled glass bowls with five-foot-high sprays of pink and white quince and placed the bowls on lightboxes, so that the flowers were illuminated from beneath and the water reflected prisms of light.

RIGHT: A plaster hand holds the label from a bottle of wine made in 1946, the year Jean Cocteau's movie *Beauty and the Beast* was released.

TOP LEFT: For after-dinner entertainment, guests go into the living room, where two glass urns, filled with quince branches, are uplit by light boxes.

LEFT MIDDLE: Quince branches, reaching to the ceiling, dominate the room.

BELOW LEFT: Trays filled with costume jewelry and copies of the book *Beauty and the Beast* are scattered as party favors throughout the apartment.

RIGHT: The urns provide dramatic accents as well as sources of illumination.

The Gardens of Versailles

■ ■ ■ ■ ■ ■ ■ ■ ■ ■ ■ ■ ■ ■ ■ ■ ■

The gardens of Versailles, landscaped with fountains, allées, parterres, and woods, were transplanted to twentieth-century Manhattan in the warm colors of autumn. In the grand design of Versailles, there are long walks, each leading to different parts of the gardens. In this party, there were also little walks, small processions, that took the guests to different sections of the "gardens," re-created in various rooms throughout the Georgian Suite, a party space on the ground floor of the apartment building where the hostess lives.

The party, to celebrate the hostess's fiftieth birthday, began with cocktails upstairs, in the home of the hostess. When the guests went downstairs for dinner, they were transported to a forest, made vivid through murals depicting the gardens of Versailles—and actual flowering trees.

The first room, which was long and narrow, was transformed into an allée of eight-foot-tall myrtle topiaries, each shaped into three balls, graduating in size. To create a sense of the eighteenth-century Orangerie, hollow oranges, each holding a votive candle, were placed at the base of the myrtles.

Orange trees, laden with natural and artificial fruit, flanked the doors to the next room. A round table, holding the placecards, was centered with a four-foot-tall obelisk topiary frame adorned with bittersweet, tuberose, and the heads of peach-colored Doris Ryker roses.

For dinner, guests were each assigned to one of three dining rooms. To enter the first, guests walked between pairs of iron garden urns filled with Japanese maple branches, pyracantha, hydrangea, viburnum, bittersweet, tuberose, and euphorbia—all in tones of cream, peach, and flame. The bittersweet curled and twisted around the pedestals, making the plant look ancient.

The three tables were covered in peach damask tablecloths fringed in peach silk. In the center of each table stood a four-foot-tall bronze candelabrum, filled with exuberant arrangements of peach-pink Oceana roses.

LEFT: In the first dining room, flowers and branches in iron garden urns and the candelabrum centerpiece create a canopy over the tables. Images of branches, projected onto the ceiling, accentuate the canopied effect.

ABOVE: The garden murals stand out as dramatic focal points in the second dining room. Lighting surrounding the cove in the ceiling backlights the fall branches in the dome, so that guests feel they are sitting under trees in a garden.

RIGHT: The pyracantha, Japanese maple, hydrangea, euphorbia, and bittersweet are radiant with the colors and textures of autumn. The tuberose adds fragrance.

■ ■ ■ ■ ■ ■ ■ ■ ■ ■

Cascading from the top of the candelabra were long vines of stephanotis, with clumps of the waxy white flowers growing along the vines. At the base of the candelabra were three miniature topiaries of myrtle in classical garlanded terra-cotta pots. The final eighteenth-century touch was the candles—three taupe-colored pillar candles, the same color as five tapers, each surrounded by a hurricane shade, which stood in the top of the candelabra.

On the walls in this dining room were three murals, painted especially for the party, that represented Versailles. The central panel depicted one of the great fountains of Versailles, while the side panels showed two allées, extending in opposite directions. The murals were painted so that they could be illuminated from behind, as if the sun were shining through the trees. Additional projection lighting created the images of lacy, shadowy leaves and branches on the ceiling.

In the next space, the dance floor, each of the four corners held a Versailles planter, a square wooden box with X-shaped sides and finials on each corner. Each planter held a fragrant orange tree, hung with fruit. At the base of each tree were more hollow oranges filled with votive candles. Still more projections of leaves and branches covered both the ceiling and floor.

In the second dining room, murals depicting large statues and columns set against fall foliage dominated the space. Just below the domed ceiling, oak and maple branches with crimson, gold, yellow, and orange leaves were suspended on wire. From these branches hung clear glass bowls filed with votive candles and tied with gold ribbons, each fastened at a different height.

ABOVE: The murals, designed by Alain Vaes, were painted with gold, yellow, and orange, and set the color tone for the room.

LEFT: Bittersweet, tuberose, and Doris Ryker roses cover a ball topiary frame. Euphorbia flowers and bittersweet berries dot the miniature myrtle topiaries.

The tablescape was a miniaturization of the parterre gardens at Versailles. A classical French urn set on a pedestal centered the tables, which were covered in fringed peach damask. Within the urn stood a single topiary frame covered with bittersweet, tuberose, and Doris Ryker roses. At the corners of the pedestal base stood miniature standard myrtle topiaries, and between these carefully sculpted topiaries were garlanded terra pots filled with full-blown roses in peach, yellow, and deep pink. Taupe pillar candles, high and low, surrounded these elements.

A mural of grand steps and balustrades leading into a garden at Versailles dominated the entire wall facing the door of the third dining room. As guests entered the room, they saw the wall as an illusionary extension of the room into another verdant space.

On the opposite walls of the room were four windows normally covered in draperies. We replaced the draperies with yet another traditional French garden material— white lattices. On the windowsills sat large iron garden urns filled with exuberant arrangements of hydrangea, roses, berried hawthorn, and viburnum branches. More bittersweet curved languidly out of the urns, and climbed on the lattice.

To heighten the sense of being in the woods in autumn, ten-foot-tall Japanese maple trees grew out of the center of each table and canopied the seated guests. From the branches hung candles tucked into glass balls and tied with gold ribbon. Encircling the trunks of the trees were garlanded terra-cotta pots overflowing with lush roses— and more taupe candles.

ABOVE: The deep pink, cream, yellow, and peach roses, all fully open, add a softer note to the colors of fall.

RIGHT: A mural covering the entire wall of the third dining room depicts a fountain at Versailles and dramatic allées. In the foreground, a Japanese maple appears to grow from the center of the table, and is surrounded by roses. Votive candles in glass balls are suspended from branches.

LEFT: The color of the peach damask tablecloths complements the color of the china, the napkins, the candles, and the flowers.

ABOVE RIGHT: Hawthorn berries, representative of autumn, nestle into the roses.

RIGHT: A trellis covers a window in the third dining room and is the background for a wild arrangement of hawthorn, roses, hydrangea, and viburnum in a wire urn. Branches of maple and oak are scattered at the base of the urn.

SCALE

■ ■

S cale is a tricky element. People are afraid of surrounding themselves with large-scale objects just as they are often fearful of bright colors. But in party design, bigger is often better. Huge centerpieces, maypoles, or banners are more dramatic than small ones. When scale is highly exaggerated, the party seems bigger than life—like theater.

For parties held in huge institutional spaces like hotel ballrooms, public libraries, or concert halls, we use scale as a design element to create a party atmosphere. We refuse to let the size of the spaces overwhelm our design.

Some rooms have the capacity for one hundred people, but also have surprisingly low ceilings. In the Radio Room atop Rockefeller Center, the view of Manhattan distracts people from the low ceilings. To keep the view completely visible, we designed very low (less than ten inches high) centerpieces.

There is yet another kind of party space, the small room with the high ceiling. In a hotel suite that seated only thirty people, the twenty-five-foot-high ceiling was disproportionate in scale. To fill that space, yet not make people feel cramped, we designed airy, sculptural canopies of flowers and vines. A similar design was used

■ ■

for a wedding in the Grand Ballroom of the Plaza Hotel in Manhattan, but because the room sat five hundred people, the canopies were heavily laden with flowers, vines, candles, and ribbons. These canopies created intimacy in the ballroom.

In spaces that have high ceilings, our design has to pierce the open space above the heads of the guests. For a party in the Grand Ballroom of the Waldorf-Astoria Hotel in Manhattan, where the ceiling is four stories high, we created a maze of streamers running from the center of each of seventy tables to the ceiling. On the promenade of the New York State Theater at Lincoln Center in New York City, where the ceilings are also forty feet high, we used twelve-foot-high heraldic banners that towered over each table.

By matching overscaled design elements to overscaled rooms, we make the guests feel not only thoroughly immersed in the ambience, but also intimately connected to other guests—once they sit down at their tables. In a small room, however, a strong graphic centerpiece focuses guests' attention on the party, and not on the architecture.

■ ■ ■ ■ ■ ■ ■ ■ ■ ■ ■

A Dinner for *Coppélia*

The lobby of the New York State Theater in Manhattan, home to the New York City Ballet, is a cold, impersonal space. One entire wall is glass, and the remaining walls and the floor are marble. Twenty-two-foot-high massive white marble sculptures of human figures flank the ends of the lobby. This institutional coldness, sometimes mistaken for grandeur, is found across the country at opera houses, symphony halls, theaters, and lobbies of office buildings. Our challenge in designing this party, a benefit for the School of American Ballet, was to find a way to warm the space.

Fabric—hundreds of yards of brocade, velvet, satin, and taffeta in such rich colors as purple, silver, emerald, gold, and fuchsia—was the answer. Fabric is soft and yielding—it can be twisted or draped in hundreds of ways—and is as warm as marble is cold.

For this party, we designed medieval heraldic banners of ten yards of fabric, which we hung, wrapped, or swathed around dark-stained wood crossbars. No two banners were alike. Then we tied French gold-wired gauze ribbon on the crossbars to add a lighthearted note, and hung cascades of red and gold cord on them.

Because the ceiling was three stories high, we designed the crossbars to stand nine and a half feet above the sixty-five tables. Some of the banners were double-sided so that they looked entirely different depending on the perspective. A purple banner was backed in fuchsia, and an emerald one in sienna. Other banners were blue or red on one side and silver on the other.

To soften the look of the banners, we wound delicate smilax vines around each vertical pole. To the smilax, we added white dendrobium orchids, which gave the banners a lacy effect.

A downward view from the balcony of the New York State Theater shows dinner tables in the lobby festooned with brilliantly colored banners. The scale of the decorations must be commensurate with the size of the space. A huge space requires equally large design elements.

ABOVE LEFT: This banner is made of voluptuously draped lengths of purple faille and silver lamé.

LEFT: A red-and-silver banner is fastened with gold rope, and a white cattleya orchid is tied with gold-wired ribbon. The wired ribbon can be twisted so that it seems to be flying in the air.

ABOVE MIDDLE: Some of the banners, like this one of turquoise taffeta, are so brilliantly colored that they can stand alone as a monochromatic design element.

ABOVE RIGHT: On the tables are white cattleya orchids nestled among smilax vines, rolled beeswax candles on clear glass plates, and crisp ecru napkins.

We had six different types of tablecloths for the sixty-five tables. Some were rose or deep burgundy cotton; a second group were silver or rose gauze, and a third group were prints. For each of the tables we mixed fabrics, sometimes folding one cloth over another. On one table, for example, we placed a silver topcloth over a rose cotton undercloth. On a second table, we used the same fabrics but folded back the silver gauze so that the table was half silver and half rose. The gauze reflected the light and the cotton absorbed it.

Because of the drama of the banners, the party space became a second stage. First, guests saw a performance on the theater stage. Then, at the party, the guests became the performers on a new stage, voluptuously wrapped.

LEFT: A twelve-foot standard, swathed in gold lamé and magenta faille, soars above a table. The rich colors complement the gold-leafed ceiling.

RIGHT: Smilax vines curl around the supports, and are topped with twists of gold-wired ribbon.

FOLLOWING PAGES: The curvilinear quality of the vines, banners, and ribbons graphically contrasts with the strong vertical and horizontal lines of the architecture.

The Most Romantic Birthday Party

At the skylit Greenhouse restaurant at the Mark Hotel in Manhattan we designed an intimate birthday party to look as if the room itself was a greenhouse and each table, with its canopy, was an eight-foot-tall tree.

The room is only twenty-four feet long and ten feet wide, although the ceiling is sixteen feet at the peak, sloping to fourteen feet. Our challenge was to make the small room dramatic.

Three sixty-inch round tables were used; the first was covered in a pink cloth, the second in peach, and the third in mauve. The colors did not clash because they were so closely related in tone, very soft and very pale. Above these pastel cloths we made the trees.

We covered each inverted canopy in ruched cotton that matched the color of the tablecloth. Ten round glass fishbowls, tied with slender peach or pink satin ribbons, were suspended from each canopy. Votive candles flickered inside the fishbowls. We also tied wired French ribbon to the arms of the canopy to give each canopy a wild, sculptural effect, as if the tree were animated and trying to spring loose from the table. We looped smilax vines around each canopy, and wired champagne roses, pale orange Mireille roses, and pink nerine lilies to the vines, which made the flowers look as if they were growing naturally. Vines trailed around the tabletop and more pale flowers were scattered among the vines.

For yet more light, there were eight fat beeswax candles, whose soft light shone through frosted hurricane lamps surrounded by more smilax vines and champagne and Mireille roses.

LEFT: For a party for thirty, each of three tables is topped by a "tree" made of shirred peach fabric, whose branches are wound with smilax vines and tied with peach, pink, and mauve wired ribbons. Round glass bowls, lit with votive candles, are suspended on ribbons. The tree fills the space above the tables, but because each tree is airy, it is never claustrophobic.

LEFT: Blush pink and ivory roses and pale pink nerines are tucked among the smilax vines at the base of the tree.

LEFT: White lily heads, champagne roses, and peach wired ribbons glimmer in the light of the candles at the crotch of a tree.

BELOW LEFT: Frosted hurricane lamps cast a warm glow along the walls of the room.

RIGHT: Candles are placed at three different heights to light the room.

The Radio Room Birthday Dinner

■ ■ ■ ■ ■ ■ ■ ■ ■ ■ ■ ■ ■ ■ ■ ■ ■

Gifts were the theme of the party for a man's fortieth birthday, held in one of Manhattan's most romantic spaces, the Radio Room, part of the Rainbow Room complex of suites on the sixty-fourth and sixty-fifth floors of Rockefeller Center.

The Radio Room celebrates the building's history as the site of NBC's radio studios in the 1940s. In the foyer, where the party began, there are Bakelite radios, pristine mementos of the '40s, carefully spaced along recessed burled wood shelves. The Art Moderne radios, in cream, maroon, and seafoam green, are treasures for collectors. The main attraction of the room, however, is not the radios but the views—of the World Trade Center towers, the Chrysler Building, and the Empire State Building to the south, and of the New Jersey shoreline and tugboats plying the Hudson River to the west. To emphasize these spectacular views, we hung triple-swagged silk balloon curtains from the five windows in the foyer, two facing west, three facing south. From each window, we suspended empty boxes wrapped in shiny metal-colored papers and tied with slender satin ribbons. A turquoise ribbon was tied around a silver gray box, an orange ribbon around a copper box, a purple ribbon around a gold box. The ribbons and papers reflected the sunlight, which poured into the room. During cocktails, the views dominated the conversation.

The dining room faces west and north, to Central Park and its reservoir. Although the view is spectacular, the room is imperfect. The rear wall has a grid pattern, on which hangs abstract art. By designing the sixty-inch round tables as brilliantly colored presents, we distracted the guests from the wall. A table covered with a turquoise cloth had a magenta bow; a purple table, a green bow; and a pale blue table, a red bow. The twelve-inch-high bows—

At this birthday party, which is in a restaurant atop Rockefeller Center in Manhattan, faux presents, wrapped in hot-pink and chartreuse paper, are suspended by ribbons.

197 ■ ■ ■ ■ ■ ■ ■ ■ ■ ■

LEFT: Each table is designed to resemble a wrapped birthday present. The centerpiece, a huge bow, can be made by sewing fabric around wire mesh for structural support.

BELOW LEFT: Each placecard is framed in silver—an alternative placecard holder.

RIGHT: In the center of each table, the bow is topped by white cattleya orchids, and multicolored paillettes are scattered around the table.

into which we tucked white cattleya orchids—were the centerpieces. Tiny white Christmas tree lights sparkled around the flowers. Placecards were inserted into silver-plated picture frames, which guests took home with them as party favors. A week or two later they received in the mail photos of themselves taken at the party.

When dinner was served, the doors to the dining room were opened. The views of the city became a backdrop for something more important—a birthday.

A Country Wedding in a Hotel Grand Ballroom

For a wedding dinner held in the Grand Ballroom of the Plaza Hotel in New York City we designed flower- and leaf-bedecked canopies that brought the outdoors indoors—and also made a large, impersonal space more intimate.

Each table had its own canopy. The center poles of the canopies were wound with smilax vines, gardenias, dendrobium orchids, and baby's breath. From the underside of the canopy we suspended white ribbons of different lengths that held the necks of tiny glass fishbowls, which, in turn, held white votive candles. At the base of each canopy, we placed three vases holding godetia, mountain laurel, and roses. The tables were covered with white moiré cloths.

To create these organic canopies, we used garden umbrellas without their canvas coverings. First we fastened sheets of chicken wire over the umbrellas with floral wire. Then we tucked sprays of lemon leaves and native smilax vines into the chicken wire, securing them with yet more floral wire. The white ribbons, which held the candles, were also tied to the chicken wire. The flowers were added last, and then we inserted the canopies into the tables.

Canopies like these, with their glistening leaves, can be used indoors or outdoors. Indoors, the smell of the flowers and the leaves seems to clean the air. A once musty hotel room suddenly smells fresh. Outdoors, especially on a hot, humid summer night, the smell of the verdant leaves and the gardenias seems to make the temperature drop.

FAR LEFT: A canopy, resembling a Victorian pergola, dominates each table at this lavish wedding reception. The graceful shape of the canopies, which envelop the guests, adds a sense of enclosure as well as fragrance.

LEFT: The canopies are made of native smilax vines entwined with masses of baby's breath and white dendrobrium orchids. White candles in glass bowls hang from the branches.

A Diplomatic Dinner

■ ■ ■ ■ ■ ■ ■ ■ ■ ■ ■ ■ ■ ■ ■ ■

When an American cabinet member dines with an Italian foreign minister, the people are the stars. The decor is merely a backdrop.

At this diplomatic dinner, protocol ruled. Like the seating, flowers were selected according to hierarchy. But just as the guests were important, the flowers had to be lush—champagne roses, peach amaryllis, and purple delphinium rather than plainer flowers.

On the twenty-sixth floor of the Beekman Towers in Manhattan, windows face the United Nations building, the East River, and midtown. The diplomats sat at the head table, which was set for nineteen. On this table we placed two baskets of pale flowers—peach tea roses, pink delphinium, white orchids, white hydrangeas shading to pink or green, peach amaryllis, and champagne roses. Purple delphinium and pointy lavender lisianthus provided shots of color. Stems were cut short, so the flowers wouldn't obscure the faces of the guests. The baskets that held the flowers were wicker painted to look like metal. The curl of the metal bows, however, subtly drew attention to the flowers.

The other thirty-one guests sat at small tables—in groups of two, four, or five—on a glass-enclosed balcony. These guests had a stunning view of the city, but not of the politicians. For these tables, we used flowers identical to those on the head table but placed them in small, low glass containers, which were more appropriate for the little tables.

The only tall arrangements were those that flanked the entrance to the dining room. As guests got off the elevator they saw two pedestals, each four and one-half feet high, with urns filled with peach-pink roses and amaryllis, interspersed with purple delphinium and white orchids. Like polite table manners, these formal arrangements of flowers were expected, designed not to overwhelm the space or the guests.

ABOVE: Pink-toned hydrangeas, white Casablanca lilies, deep blue delphinium, lavender scabiosa, and champagne and pink roses compose the centerpieces on the balcony tables.

RIGHT: In this dramatic penthouse space, silver plates, along with the mirrors, reflect every glimmer of light.

An "Artful" Birthday Party

What does an all-white modern art gallery with a thirty-foot-high ceiling need to host a rock-and-roll birthday party?

The answer is brilliant color on a huge scale. Austere, minimalist spaces seldom make people want to dance with abandon. After all, rock and roll wasn't born in a convent.

For this party for 120 people we placed twelve tables around an empty space in the middle of the gallery, creating a dance floor. Each table was designed in primary colors. The inverted canopies, which towered eight feet above the floor, were either red, orange, yellow, blue, or green. A table with a red canopy had a yellow tablecloth and green chairs; an orange canopy had a blue tablecloth and yellow chairs.

From the four corners of each canopy hung glass fishbowls, which held white votive candles, and wired French ribbons in red, yellow, pink, green, and blue. At the center of the table white cattleya orchids nestled among more jagged twists of wired ribbon. At each place setting, there were glass napkin rings that doubled as tiny bud vases. Each ring held one or two flowers, either pink, yellow, or white tulips, white or yellow freesias, or tender lavender sweet peas.

The center of the gallery, with its great bolts of color, was the focal point of the party. The art hanging on the walls was a pleasant distraction, an excuse to have a quiet conversation away from the music. But the heart of the party was around and on the dance floor. With the music blaring, people really cut loose.

Red, yellow, blue, and green canopies—with white candles in glass bowls hanging from the corners—fill this high-ceilinged white art gallery with color and light. When ceilings are high, canopies are a good choice to fill empty volumes of space.
The chairs and napkins are also red, yellow, blue, and green. Each napkin is tucked into a glass napkin ring that doubles as a vase.

A Traditional Hospital Benefit

When faced with a modest budget, such as the one for this hospital benefit at the Waldorf-Astoria, we chose curly willow branches, common flowers of late summer, and ribbons. The willow branches were large, sculptural, yet inexpensive. The ribbons cost little. And the flowers—zinnias, dahlias, hydrangeas, and lilies—were locally grown.

The enormous centerpieces, which soared five to six feet above the tables, helped to fill the volume of overhead space and became airy canopies that hovered gently over the guests. Some of the branches were as tall as seven feet.

The tables were covered in peach damask cloths over pink moiré undercloths. To harmonize with the peach-pink background we chose flowers that ranged in color from white to pink to coral to deep red.

Each bouquet combined at least three of the four flowers mentioned above. One vase held lilies in three colors—burgundy, deep pink, and yellow—and white hydrangeas. Another vase held a bouquet of darker tones—coral dahlias, coral lilies, and white hydrangeas. Yet another vase held purple hydrangeas shading to lavender, red lilies, and orange zinnias.

To prevent the room from looking too pastel, the ribbons were red, purple, green, orange, and yellow. Each willow branch held sixteen to twenty ribbons, each cut twelve to sixteen inches long. Some curled at the bottom. The fat hydrangeas, the focal point of each bouquet, contrasted with the slender ribbons.

In scale with the large room, there were two large urns holding yellow crab apple branches, hydrangeas, delphinium, goldenrod, lilies, celosia, and curly willow—the largest and boldest we could find.

White hydrangeas, peach and pink roses, and curly willow branches tied with long, trailing ribbons extend from tall glass vases in the center of each table.

Fête de Mai

■ ■ ■ ■ ■ ■ ■ ■ ■ ■ ■ ■ ■ ■ ■

In Europe, since the Middle Ages, people have celebrated the first of May by dancing around maypoles garlanded with flowers and streamers. In France, where romance has been cultivated as an art, the first of May is celebrated through the simple but touching ritual of men giving women bouquets of lilies of the valley. So for Fête de Mai, a lavish benefit for the New York City Ballet held in the Grand Lobby of the New York State Theater at Lincoln Center in Manhattan, we combined elements of these two ancient rituals—maypoles and lilies of the valley. On this evening, partygoers—including members of the New York City Ballet—danced until two in the morning.

The two maypoles, which were twenty-four feet high, were the soaring focal points of the room, which held seventy tables. Medieval maypoles were rigid poles garlanded with fresh flowers and wrapped in lengths of fabric, which the dancers held. Our maypoles were made of lengths of iridescent fabric in shades of magenta, lavender, and pink, which were twisted and draped so the colors intertwined. To create the illusion that the poles were decorated with flowers we wound garlands of fresh laurel leaves down the length of the maypole. Every four feet, we tied the maypole with floppy bows of five-inch-wide silk satin ribbon that was blue shading to lavender. Wherever we tied a ribbon bow, we also pinned plump bunches of fake hydrangeas that were a pale blush pink. We crowned the top of the maypole with ostrich plumes in four shades of pink, ranging from hot Schiaparelli pink to pearl pink. Gold-wired ribbon created sculptural arabesques around the feathers. From the tops of the maypoles five-foot-wide streamers in lavender, pink, hot pink, and pale pink reached to the sides of the balconies. In all, over five hundred yards of fabric were used.

Since the maypoles weren't solidly anchored to the floor, we had to stabilize them through sleight of hand. We tied aircraft cable around the top of each maypole, just under the feather crown, and tied the ends of the cable to the rails

ABOVE: Maypoles add a lighthearted note to the stark, modern architecture of the cavernous space of the New York State Theater.

RIGHT: Two maypoles, made of long lengths of pink and fuchsia fabric that were gathered and tied with flowers, are the focal point of the space.

ABOVE: A balcony view of the formal and precisely set tables, with pointed white napkins, a symmetrical ring of candles, and gold and dark green chairs. Tables should have enough distance between them so that chairs don't have to be tucked underneath. This leaves the cloth hanging straight, with a natural fall to the floor.

of the balconies twenty-four feet above the floor. At the bottom of the maypoles, we placed sandbags on the swaths of fabric and then bunched up the remaining yards of fabric to cover the sandbags. From the balconies pale pink spotlights washed over the room, making all the fabrics look warm but not flashy.

Just as the maypoles were the focal points of the room, a topiary of glossy boxwood leaves and white lilies of the valley was the centerpiece of each table. The round topiaries were perched on white birch trunks and were highlighted by the seventy spotlights we placed on the balconies and ceiling—one light for each topiary. To balance this light we placed seven beeswax candles, each two inches in diameter, on each table to cast a soft, flickering uplight.

The tablecloths echoed the springtime theme of flowers. Made of beige linen, the round cloths were printed with bouquets of pale and dusky pink roses and peonies, which were gaily linked by garlands of lavender ropes. Chairs were gold with beige cushions.

Since the benefit was for the ballet, the dancers were invited to eat and dance—but their tables were on the balcony, overlooking the guests. For the dancers, we swagged the railings of the balcony with garlands of fresh laurel. On each of the dancers' tables we placed a silver candelabrum that held four white tapers, cascades of purple and green grapes, and white cattleya orchids. In the first part of the evening, when the dancers performed, they were the ones being watched. At dinner, the dancers were the observers, the audience the observed.

ABOVE: Garlands of smilax, magenta and pink fabric, hydrangeas, and roses drape the balcony. To keep the hydrangeas and roses fresh, the flowers are discreetly tucked into glass water tubes.

ABOVE RIGHT: For drama, theatrical spotlights focus on the tops of the maypoles.

RIGHT: Wide ribbons of fabric alternate with lengths of fabric that are braided with native smilax vines, hydrangeas, and dendrobium orchids.

ABOVE: Finials of hot-pink ostrich plumes top the maypoles.

LEFT: Boxwood topiaries, dotted with lilies of the valley, perch on thick birch trucks that rest in Italian stone pots.

RIGHT: Ribbons shading from light to dark tones tie bouquets of flowers together.

Puttin' on the Ritz

■ ■ ■ ■ ■ ■ ■ ■ ■ ■ ■ ■ ■ ■ ■ ■ ■ ■

Any room with a low eight-to-ten-foot-high ceiling can feel oppressive, whether it's a modern corporate dining room with a low acoustical ceiling, a hotel convention room, or a dining room at home. On the other hand, a room with a high ceiling can be intimidating. At a dinner dance for four hundred people at the Ritz, a theater in Manhattan, we were confronted with both problems. The dining area had a low ceiling, only ten feet high. The dance floor, however, was under a domelike fifty-foot ceiling. To unite these contrasting spaces, we designed a bold black-and-white scheme so graphic and powerful that you forgot about the architecture. Although there was a theme—"Puttin' on the Ritz"—it was the stark black and white that transformed the space.

The dining area, which held forty tables, was tucked under the balconies and contributed to the feeling of claustrophobia. Worse, the walls flanking the dining area were lined with emergency exit doors, whose signs glowed red. The dance area was in front of the stage.

We covered the tables with alternating black and white tablecloths. On tables with white cloths, the napkins, chairs, and paillettes were black. Conversely, on tables with black cloths the napkins and chairs were white, the paillettes silver.

In the dining area the centerpieces, which were over five feet high, helped unify the space. We filled two-foot-high silver candelabra with four thirty-inch-high white tapers, sprays of white dendrobium orchids, and delicate white ostrich plumes. Not only did the candelabra focus attention on the center of the table, but they also masked the view of the ceiling and the fire exit signs. Votive candles provided uplight. The paillettes glimmered with reflected light. Looking across the room, the guests saw only the candelabra and their fellow celebrants. The balconies, ceiling, and walls seemed to disappear.

ABOVE: The black-and-white theme of this occasion is echoed in the way the party favors are wrapped.

RIGHT: To focus attention on the centers of the tables, masses of tall candelabra provided the main light source in this cavernous and incohesive theater space. For the party, the floor is covered with overscaled black-and-white checkerboard tiles.

The dance area posed the opposite problem: the ceiling was high, the space vast. To complement the large-scale space, we designed an overscaled checkerboard dance floor. Each black and white Masonite square was four feet by four feet and was attached to the floor with two strips of double-faced tape. To animate this huge space we hung a twenty-by-twenty-foot white projection screen against a black theatrical drop and showed clips from the delectable Fred Astaire and Ginger Rogers movies made by RKO in the 1930s.

The boldness of the black-and-white scheme—the large centerpieces, the movie screen, and the oversized checkerboard squares—dominated the space. The theme was obvious—it could not be missed.

Don't Bungle the Jungle

When a room such as Lepercq Space at the Brooklyn Academy of Music has no more charm than a garage or a warehouse, you try to make the room disappear. Here, at a party benefiting Don't Bungle the Jungle, a group committed to preserving the Amazon rain forest, art inspired the design and happily predominated over the setting.

Artist Kenny Scharf, famous for his '50s-inspired "Jetson" paintings of pointy-headed people and satellites whirling around in outer space, was the chairman of the benefit. For the room, which measured 125 feet long by forty-five wide, with a thirty-two-foot-high ceiling, he painted a whimsical backdrop that was as large as it was amusing. The canvas backdrop, which measured twenty-five feet high by forty feet wide, depicted a fifteen-foot-high flirtatious green and yellow butterfly with long eyelashes that asked to be batted—and who wore high heels. The image was Betty Boop as butterfly. Around the butterfly, Scharf painted dense twisting and curving green vines, red flowers, and a yellow snake that wrapped itself around a tree trunk, eyeing the butterfly. In this forest beauty and fragility coexisted with danger.

Since the room was enormous, we designed huge canopies that measured six feet across and soared five feet above each table. The canopies, similar to those used in tropical countries to ward off the sun, echoed the primeval jungle theme of the backdrop. To make these canopies, we used four-armed canopy frames as the structure, and placed one pole in the center hole of each table. We wrapped 120-inch round cloths—which Scharf had painted peach, yellow, or white with green, blue, black, or red squiggles—around the poles, whose arms extended upward at a forty-five-degree angle. We tied the cloth to the end of each arm using green nylon monofilament (so the tying wouldn't be noticeable). We gathered the cloth at the top and stapled it together. Since the cloth collapsed a little in the middle, no one saw the staples.

ABOVE: Sometimes, paper flowers (in this case, sixteen inches in diameter) can be more effective than natural flowers because of their size and color. The idea is *not* to imitate reality!

RIGHT: Artist Kenny Scharf painted canvas canopies and various other colorful backdrops for this lively benefit party. An inflatable snake slithers up the center pole of this canopy, while pterodactyls look down.

LEFT AND ABOVE: The asymmetrical canopies are covered with fanciful abstract designs and imaginative fauna, the focal points in an otherwise dark space.

The rain forest is home to rare, lush flowers; on the canopies, magenta, lemon yellow, turquoise, orange, and purple crepe-paper flowers bloomed. We wired flowers to the corners of the canopies, or entwined them around the poles. Then we wrapped the laundry poles with inflated plastic pterodactyls, snakes, and tyrannosaurs, in the spirit of Scharf's painting.

By spotlighting the backdrop and the canopies, and keeping the rest of the space dark, the scale of these lighted elements focused the guests' attention to the point of the benefit.

The April in Paris Ball

■ ■ ■ ■ ■ ■ ■ ■ ■ ■ ■ ■ ■ ■ ■ ■ ■ ■ ■

When a ceiling soars, a space can feel magnificent, whether it's a drawing room in a nineteenth-century Victorian house, a dining room in a country club, or a ballroom. However, in a high-ceilinged room, you can also feel lost, dwarfed, and intimidated. The trick, then, for a fabulous party, is to fill that vast expanse of space so that people feel joyous and connected to their surroundings—not lonely and alienated.

The Grand Ballroom of the Waldorf-Astoria Hotel in New York City is like many hotel ballrooms across the country—only grander. The ceiling is fifty feet high; the room is one hundred feet square; and the stage, which is the main focus of the room, is sixty feet wide. The space is designed to accommodate hundreds of people. It is easy for a large party to fragment into uneasy clusters unless some coherence is brought to the cavernous space.

To make the high-ceilinged space warm (this size space can never be made entirely intimate), we filled the ballroom with sixty-foot-long streamers made of lavender, hot pink, and mint green gauze, colors that suited the function, the April in Paris Ball. The theme was "Joie de Vivre," so we chose the lighthearted colors of spring's first flowers—the pale green of early leaves, the pink of tulips, and lavender of crocuses. These colors were echoed in the tablecloths and in the soft gathering of sheer fabric in the center of the tables. If a banner was mint green, the tablecloth might be hot pink, and the fluff of fabric in the center lavender. Usually a room filled with round tables has a heavy, oppressive feeling because of the mass of tablecloths and chairs. But here, the colors lightened up the atmosphere.

The streamers pierced the air, filling the space with bolts of color and joining the seventy-four tables together. To further warm the room, we tied streamers to the chandeliers and secured them to the center of each table. We also ran streamers from the highest balcony railing to

the center of the table. Because the banners crisscrossed in the air, the room looked lively, not static.

For each banner, there was a separate spotlight, which was attached to the balcony. The lights zeroed in on the center of each table, following the angle of the banner. To balance the spotlights there were tiny battery-charged white Christmas tree lights tucked under the fluffy fabric in the center of the table. These lights cast a soft glow from under the fabric and highlighted the flowers scattered in the center of the table. White votive candles added a golden light.

Since the banners filled the room with color, the flowers—gardenias and cattleya orchids—were pristinely white for contrast. We tucked each flower into a glass vial filled with water and hid the vials in the mounds of fabric. Finally, we sprinkled silver paillettes the size of quarters around the table, so that even more light danced off the table.